UNCOVERING
GOD'S WORD

women♥offaith™

UNCOVERING
GOD'S WORD

BY

CHRISTA KINDE

FOREWORD BY

LUCI SWINDOLL

THOMAS NELSON
Since 1798

Published in Nashville, Tennessee, by Thomas Nelson.
Thomas Nelson is a trademark of HarperCollins Christian Publishing, Inc.

Thomas Nelson books may be purchased in bulk for educational, business, fundraising, or sales promotional use. For information, please e-mail SpecialMarkets@ ThomasNelson.com.

Scripture quotations marked NKJV are taken from *The Holy Bible*, The New King James Version (NKJV®). Copyright © 1979, 1980, 1982, Thomas Nelson, Inc. Publishers. Used by permission. All rights reserved.

Scripture quotations marked ncv are taken from *The Holy Bible*, The New Century Version®. Copyright © 1987, 1988, 1991 by Word Publishing, a Division of Thomas Nelson, Inc. Used by permission. All rights reserved.

Scripture quotations marked NLT are taken from *The Holy Bible*, The New Living Translation (NLT). Copyright © 1986 by the Tyndale House Publishers, Wheaton, Illinois, 60189. Used by permission. All rights reserved.

Scripture quotations marked MSG are taken from *The Holy Bible*, The Message (MSG), Copyright © 1993. Used by permission of NavPress Publishing Group.

Other books referenced in this work include NKJV Study Bible, Nelson's New Illustrated Bible Commentary, and the Believer's Bible Commentary. Published by Thomas Nelson Publishers. Used by permission.

ISBN: 978-0-3106-8265-3

First Printing May 2016 / Printed in the United States of America

⫸ CONTENTS ⫷

FOREWORD

At the age of ten I decided to run away from home. I remember that morning when I took a little suitcase off the top shelf of my closet and began packing it with what I needed most—a few clothes, a few books, a few toys and my favorite scrapbook from "Momo", my grandmother. As I was making progress, my dad walked by the door, saw what I was doing and came in. He sat on the end of the bed.

"What's up?" he asked.

"I'm leaving, daddy. I don't want to live here anymore".

He looked at me very calmly. "Okay . . . but what happened that made you want to do this?", pointing to my suitcase. He was genuinely concerned . . . ever so sweet and eager to know what had upset me.

"I never get to do anything my way. I don't like the food here. I'm sick of always having to mind. There are too many rules. It's a bunch of stuff . . . so I'm running away". My voice was cracking.

"I see. But where will you eat?" he asked. "Who will love you when you're sick? What will you do when you run out of money?"

I reminded him I had my $2.00 allowance.

"Two dollars won't go very far, honey," he said. "But, if you're determined to go, I'll help you pack. In fact, I'll go with you."

That was worse! Daddy wants me to go, I thought . . . or he wouldn't offer to help. It was a very confusing moment; I was stuck in a dilemma and needed something to change but I didn't know what. I just wanted relief from my childish predicament and thought running away would do it. After talking with my dad for a while though, and having him receive me where I was, I felt better and finally settled down and unpacked.

About fifteen years later I remember having those same feelings. Only, this time they were from the spiritual side of me, not the physical. I was sick of my life as it was— tired of obeying the rules; unhappy with the food I was eating and never getting to do what I wanted. Truthfully, I thought of running away. But where would I go? I was twenty-five, a college graduate, in the work force and getting established as an adult, albeit an immature one.

Through a chain of events I found myself in a Bible class where I began to learn the truth of God's Word. Four nights a week for two years I listened to a godly, knowledgeable, brilliant teacher explain the scriptures in a way I had never understood before. It was wonderful. Little by little, my life began to take on new meaning and depth. I stopped just reading the Bible and started studying it. I learned how to apply God's promises to different situations; how to appropriate doctrine to my experience so I didn't have to make decisions based on feelings. I began a scripture memory program and immediately noticed the value of having God's Word in my heart so it came to mind at a moment's notice. In short, I was a sponge searching for the River of life . . . and when I found it in Bible study I sat down and soaked it up. Nothing in my life—NOTHING—has ever mattered to me as much as those two years of study. That teaching has come to my aid every day of my life since I was twenty-five.

This little book, *Knowing God's Word Study Guide* is that kind of resource. It will help you understand the reason you need to learn Scripture by heart and recall it every day. It will tell you what's important in life and what isn't. It will encourage you to have goals that are not only right, but also righteous. It will start at the basics and lead you to maturity as a Christian. It will teach you there's a warm, loving home to go to when you want to run away. It will be the relief you need from life's predicaments.

And most important, when you're fed up and ready to throw in the towel this Study Guide will show you how your Father . . . the God of The Bible . . . is there for you, loving you when you're sick, providing for you when you're broke, receiving you as you are and offering to go the distance with you all the way to the end.

Nothing is more important than knowing God's Word. It's the River of life. You're the sponge. Sit down and soak it up.

—Luci Swindoll

⤣ INTRODUCTION ⤤

For many people, the thought of studying brings back unpleasant memories of school. Those were the days when we were told what we needed to know. We endured lectures, library-time, projects, and pop quizzes. Homework was the scourge of our young lives—dull, daily, and always due. We only learned what we needed to know for the test. We retained our knowledge just long enough to secure a passing grade, then promptly forgot it all. None of us really expected to need to know algebra outside of high school. And when we finally scraped our way through our senior year and across the graduation platform, we were determined never to open another textbook again.

Of course that's not everyone's experience. But still, most people retain the notion that learning takes place in the classroom, and when you're through with school, you're through with "book learning." And of course, that's not really the case. We can and do learn, and we needn't enroll in a class to do it. With a basic understanding of the tools we need and a willingness to apply ourselves to our studies, we can enjoy a lifetime of learning.

This Bible study has a two-fold purpose. First, it is designed to teach us how to study the Scriptures. It introduces us to the tools and techniques we need to know. And secondly, while we're learning how to study the Bible, we'll be learning all about what the Bible tells us about itself. This will give us a hands-on approach. We'll be learning something while we learn how to learn! Interested? I think this is going to be fun. Let's go!

Be diligent to present yourself approved to God, a worker who does not need to be ashamed, rightly dividing the word of truth.

2 Timothy 2:15 NKJV

CHAPTER ONE

WILL THIS BE ON THE TEST?

"FROM CHILDHOOD YOU HAVE KNOWN THE HOLY SCRIPTURES, WHICH ARE ABLE TO MAKE YOU WISE."

2 Timothy 3:15 NKJV

The student's worst nightmare seems to be finding oneself in a life-and-death situation, only to find out the arcane tidbits we ignored while we were in school are now vital to our survival. It's like the Far Side® cartoon that puts some poor soul outside Peter's gate, and the only way to gain entry is by solving a complex algebra equation. Or another cartoon I've seen where a man is held at gunpoint, and asked, "If a train leaves a station in Chicago, and is traveling at 60 MPH, and another train leaves at that same time from San Francisco, traveling at 45 MPH . . . ." You get the idea.

The reason these comics are so humorous is that they're so far-fetched. Very few of us actually need algebra on a daily basis. And so we laugh at it. It's impractical. Who really cares? Ah, but what if you're involved in one of the many sciences that depends upon such mathematical equations as regularly as breathing? Would you mock the math then? No! In fact, you'd take it quite seriously.

CLEARING ↗ THE ↖ COBWEBS

What was your by-far, no-question, totally least favorite class when you were in school?

> We have the opportunity to learn from life or to ignore its teaching.
>
> Nicole Johnson

Your grasp of such principles and your accuracy in computing them would affect your very livelihood. So you see, algebra is only impractical if you don't need it. But for those who use it every day, it's absolutely necessary.

We're believers. Our lives are based on the truths of Scripture. For us, they're absolutely necessary. We take them seriously because they aren't arcane tidbits or interesting little factoids. The Scriptures are God's revelation to us—His Word. By them we know God, and by them we were saved.

1. Let's ask a few questions here:

• What's absolutely vital for living the Christian life?

• Where can we find out about who God is and what He's like?

- How can we know what God expects of us?

- Where can we find real truth?

- What is the only source of true prophecies?

- What is our best source of daily comfort, encouragement, and wisdom?

> *Remember that God is in the business of building our characters, not our empires.*
> Luci Swindoll

> *All day long God longs for our company. All day long God longs to show us mercy.*
>
> Sheila Walsh

2. According to 2 Timothy 3:15, what are the Scriptures able to do in our lives?

3. So if the Bible is so vital for faith, why don't we spend more time reading it? Can we be honest here—do any of these words describe how you feel about reading the Scriptures?

- ❏ Boring
- ❏ Uninteresting
- ❏ Bewildering
- ❏ Over my head
- ❏ Tedious
- ❏ Dull
- ❏ Perplexing
- ❏ Outdated
- ❏ Confusing
- ❏ Mind-numbing

- ❏ Intimidating
- ❏ Impractical
- ❏ Unapproachable
- ❏ Archaic
- ❏ Offensive
- ❏ Tiresome
- ❏ Unreadable
- ❏ Daunting
- ❏ Monotonous
- ❏ Incomprehensible

4. Well then, how about studying? Even if we spend time reading our Bibles, why don't we take more time to study the Scriptures? Do any of these reasons ring a bell?

❑ I'm not smart enough.

❑ I don't know where to start.

❑ I don't have a place to study.

❑ I don't have time.

❑ I might be wrong.

❑ I'll leave that to my pastor.

❑ I wouldn't know how to do it correctly.

❑ I don't have the training.

❑ I don't have any resources.

ibles. They come in all shapes and sizes these days. There are many translations. There are many styles. There are even many colors. They come with study notes, cross-references, timelines, devotionals, and commentary. They're in hotel lobbies and hospital waiting rooms. Every hotel room in America has one in a bedside table. Most Christians have a handful of them laying around the house somewhere. They're so commonplace, so readily available, that I think we sometimes forget just what we hold in our hands.

5. Let's begin our study with one of the most amazing passages in all of Scripture. John 1:1–5. What does this passage tell us about the relationship between God and the Word?

> In the beginning was the Word, and the Word was with God, and the Word was God. He was in the beginning with God. All things were made through Him, and without Him nothing was made that was made. In Him was life, and the life was the light of men. And the light shines in the darkness, and the darkness did not comprehend it. —John 1:1–5 NKJV

6. Okay. It's time to access your very first Bible study tool—cross-references. Just about every Bible has them. And these are a simple way to find verses that "go together." Let's start with John 1:1. My Bible cross-references three verses. Look them up, and write down how they broaden our understanding of John 1:1:

John 17:5 –

1 John 1:1 –

Revelation 19:13 –

7. If we read a bit further in John 1, we come across a very enlightening verse. What does John 1:14 tell us about the Word?

> ## DID YOU NOTICE?
>
> *Isn't it interesting that the three verses used to cross-reference John 1:1 were also written by John—the beloved disciple? John wrote five books of the New Testament—the Gospel of John, 1 John, 2 John, 3 John, and Revelation. One of the ways in which scholars determine the authorship of a book of the Bible is by similarities of style and vocabulary. Obviously, referring to Jesus as "The Word" is characteristic of John's writings.*

Let's sum up what we've discovered so far:

- John refers to Jesus as the Word.
- Jesus was with God before time began.
- Jesus is God.
- Jesus shares in the glory of God.
- Jesus became a man who could be seen, heard, and touched.
- Jesus is called the Word of life.
- One of Jesus' names is the Word of God.
- Jesus is coming again.

All of these truths gleaned from just one verse and its cross-references. Sometimes that's what we do when we study—pull together a list of what we've learned.

8. Now let's look at the cross-reference for John 1:3—Colossians 1:16–17.

9. When we want to be certain of the meaning of a statement in Scripture, we look for other verses that verify it. It is best to let Scripture define itself. Take a look at each of these verses, which take up the thread we started in John 1:3:

- Hebrews 11:3

- 2 Peter 3:5

- Psalm 33:6

DIGGING DEEPER

When you're choosing a Bible for study, there are two basic routes you can take. One is to find a good study Bible. There are many, many study Bibles available to you in your local Christian bookstores, but a good standard, from which we'll be quoting throughout this study is the NKJV Study Bible from Thomas Nelson. Study Bibles give notes and commentary on the Scriptures, helping you to understand what you're reading. The second route to take in Bible study is to find a Bible without many notes, but with plenty of space in which you can make your own notes as you go along. This allows you to jot down questions, make note of cross-references, and even take sermon notes right in your Bible. An excellent Bible for this purpose is NKJV Note-Taker's Bible.

PONDER & PRAY

This week pray for a heart prepared to learn. Ask the Lord to lead you as you read through the Scriptures. Pray for an inquisitive nature, as you slow down and consider the meaning behind the various words and phrases you know so well. And pray that your studies will not become a mere accumulation of facts. Instead, ask that the Holy Spirit could help you to see how the things you learn can change your heart.

TRINKETS TO TREASURE

At the close of each lesson, you will be presented with a small gift. Though imaginary, it will serve to remind you of the things you have learned. Think of it as a souvenir. Souvenirs are little trinkets we pick up on our journeys to remind us of where we have been. They keep us from forgetting the path we have traveled. Hide these little treasures in your heart, for as you ponder them, they will draw you closer to God.

The Bible we hold in our hands is the very Word of God. We read it with joy, we study it with fascination. This week, your trinket will be something absolutely necessary in your study of the Scriptures—a pencil. Never read your Bible without a pencil in your hand! That way, you can make notes, jot down questions, underline key words. We read, not to check off a daily task, but to understand God's revelation of Himself to His people. A sharpened pencil in our hand will help to keep our mind sharp as well!

NOTES & PRAYER REQUESTS

CHAPTER TWO

TOOLS OF THE TRADE

"OF MAKING MANY BOOKS THERE IS NO END, AND MUCH STUDY IS WEARISOME TO THE FLESH."

Ecclesiastes 12:12 NKJV

Some of the most clever ads I've seen are memorable because they're so silly. They picture men and women doing an everyday task but with an absurdly inappropriate tool. You wouldn't slice bread with a chainsaw. You wouldn't use a leaf-blower to dry your hair. You wouldn't comb through your hair with a rake. You wouldn't trim your toenails with hedge clippers. You need the right tool for the right job.

Now when it comes down to the nitty-gritty of Bible study, you need the proper tools for the job as well. And before you dash out to your local neighborhood Christian bookstore, you need to have some idea just what each of these resources can do for you. Let's give them a quick run-down.

CLEARING ⚞ THE ⚟ COBWEBS

Do you have a hobby of some sort? What is the most essential tool of your trade within that favorite pastime?

Cross-references—We've already mentioned those handy little notes that appear in our Bibles. Whether you've got a center column reference or your cross-references appear after each verse, they point you to related Scriptures found elsewhere in the Bible.

Study Bible—A study Bible has notes on the bottom of each page. In essence, these are a commentary, placed side-by-side with our Bible text. You can get study Bibles on all kinds of themes these days. The NKJV Study Bible is a good standard, but there are many others.

Devotional Bible—These Bibles have daily readings so that you can combine your scripture readings with a devotional thought. For instance, the *Women of Faith® Devotional Bible* covers twelve different themes over the course of the year, with readings for every day of the month written by the speakers and friends of Women of Faith®.

> *How fortunate we are that we don't even need a telephone to reach Him.*
>
> Barbara Johnson

Topical Bible—This resource arranges Bible topics in alphabetical order, giving each one a comprehensive list of Bible verses in which the topic is dealt with throughout Scripture. I often use *The MacArthur Topical Bible*, and it's absolutely invaluable for Bible study!

Biblical Cyclopedic Index—Some Bibles, like *The Open Bible*, have an abbreviated version of a Topical Bible right in the front. Very handy!

Bible Concordance—This is an alphabetical listing of every use of every word found in Scriptures along with the passage in which it is found. *Strong's Exhaustive Concordance of the Bible* is the standard.

Bible Dictionary—We all love Webster's, but there are some words that just don't turn up in an average dictionary. A Bible dictionary defines those terms that we run across as we study, and defines them in the light of the Scriptures.

A to Z™ Resources—These are more contemporary reference tools, but they can come in handy while doing Bible research. *Where to Find It in the Bible* and *Find it Fast in the Bible* are both available.

Bible Handbook—A Bible handbook gives you an overview of the Bible. It's the condensed version, summarizing the theme of each chapter in the Bible. This helps you get a grasp on the big picture and the themes of Scripture.

Commentary—A Bible commentary can turn what seems like complicated theology into practical understanding. Going phrase by phrase, and sometimes word by word, through the Scriptures, a commentary helps you understand what the Bible means.

To the man who pleases him, God gives wisdom, knowledge and happiness.
Ecclesiastes 2:26 NIV

Biblical Encyclopedias—Since there is a lot of ground to cover, most Bible Encyclopedias come in multiple volumes. However, they are able to give more exhaustive descriptions of the topics we find in our Bibles, making them excellent for doing background research.

Expository Dictionary—These are also called Word Study Dictionaries. *Vine's Expository Dictionary* is an excellent example of this type of resource. They help us to understand what a word meant in its original language, with all the connotations and associations that would have been apparent to believers in the time they were written.

Manners & Customs—These are the books that take us back into Bible times and tell us what it was like to live back then. They cover everything from clothes and food to festivals and traditions.

Interlinear—When it comes down to roll-up-your-sleeves and dabble in the original languages time, you'll probably want to hunt up an Interlinear. This book lays out the Greek text on the page, then gives you the literal English translation of those words underneath.

I recall all you have done, O LORD; I remember your wonderful deeds of long ago.
Psalm 77:11 NLT

Parallel Bible—Parallel Bibles put two or more texts side by side, so that you can compare them as you read. Some Parallel Bibles compare two different translations.

Atlas—We're talking maps here! Most atlases will have ancient maps as well as modern ones. Some will have overlays, satellite imagery, and smaller maps of things like the tabernacle and Solomon's temple.

Bible Software—Computers are amazing, and if you're technologically inclined, you can have all the above resources and more installed on your home computer.

Now take a moment and consider how these different resources could help you in your Bible study. Let's go back to the verse we ended with last week—2 Timothy 3:16–17.

"All Scripture is given by inspiration of God, and is profitable for doctrine, for reproof, for correction, for instruction in righteousness, that the man of God may be complete, thoroughly equipped for every good work" (NKJV).

1. What can you learn about these four terms used in 2 Timothy 3:16 from the notes you have in a study Bible?

Doctrine –

Reproof –

Correction –

Instruction –

2. Look up "inspiration" in your Bible concordance. Is it used anywhere else in the Bible?

3. Now find a commentary, and research the literal meaning of the word translated "inspiration" in 2 Timothy 3:16. What is it?

4. Let's do a little word study here. Find an expository dictionary, like *Vine's Expository Dictionary*, and see if you can dig up the meaning of "complete," as it is used in 2 Timothy 3:17.

5. All right, what can you find out about "thoroughly equipped"?

6. All this study and preparation lead up to one thing—good works. What does the topical Bible say about this subject?

*N*ow let's turn you loose on a couple of verses. Gather up as many resources as you can. If you don't have many books at home, check out your church's library. The more reference works and commentaries you explore, the broader your understanding will be. Spend the rest of the week carefully going over these two verses, which speak of the Word of God as a sword. Take notes on what you have learned.

"And take the helmet of salvation, and the sword of the Spirit, which is the word of God." —Ephesians 6:17 NKJV

"For the word of God is living and powerful, and sharper than any two-edged sword, piercing even to the division of the soul and spirit, and of joints and marrow, and is a discerner of the thoughts and intents of the heart." —Hebrews 4:12 NKJV

Digging Deeper

Often, when you are reading or studying your Bible, you'll have a moment of clarity, an epiphany, or a brilliant thought that you don't want to forget. Other times, you'll have a troubling question, which you'll want to hang onto until you can get to your books or your trusted friends to talk it through. In these cases, your best friend is a sticky-note. Keep slim piles of sticky-notes stuck in the back of your Bible. Then they'll always be close at hand.

Ponder & Pray

God appreciates our thanks, even for the small things in life. Why not thank Him today for the things that help to make Bible study a joy for you. Pink highlighters? Little star-shaped sticky-notes? Green colored pencils? A wide-margin Bible? Your new leather journal? And while you're at it, thank God for those who have paved the way for your studies—the translators, editors, and authors of reference works. God has used their diligent work to touch your life!

Trinkets to Treasure

This week your trinket to treasure is another invaluable study aid—the humble sticky-note! These days we can find them in all shapes, sizes, and colors. Though one of the lesser tools of the Bible study trade, they have their place, marking pages and capturing thoughts. Tuck your new batch in the back of your Bible, where they'll always be close at hand.

NOTES & PRAYER REQUESTS

READING VS. STUDYING

"THEY RECEIVED THE WORD WITH ALL READINESS,
AND SEARCHED THE SCRIPTURES DAILY TO FIND
OUT WHETHER THESE THINGS WERE SO."

Acts 17:11 NKJV

Have you ever wondered why reading the Bible is so different from reading a novel? When we've got a real page-turner in our hands, with an exciting plot and interesting characters, we can read all day long as the story unfolds. Yet when it comes to Scripture, we get bogged down after a couple of pages. We feel guilty because we can't get the same mileage we do with fiction.

Here's the thing—the novels we pick up for light reading are fun, relaxing diversions. Our thoughts are entertained by the story. But when we read our Bibles, there's a subtle shift that takes place. Our minds must be engaged when we read Scripture. That means giving the words on the page our full concentration. That takes time. Our spirit responds to the Word of God in a way that cannot be taken lightly. Our goal is not recreation, but comprehension. We want to understand

CLEARING THE COBWEBS

Have you ever tried one of those read-through-the-Bible-in-a-year programs?

what we're reading, and so we take it slowly. We may feel guilty that we can't cover several pages in one sitting, but what is our goal—distance or discernment?

1. When we read our Bibles, we are reading for understanding. That might mean rereading a verse several times, or chasing after several cross-references, or referring to a commentary in order to grasp the writer's meaning. Match up these verses, which declare the importance of gaining understanding:

____ Job 32:8   a. Give me understanding so I can know Your Word.

____ Psalm 119:34   b. Understanding is to be chosen over silver.

____ Psalm 119:125   c. Apply your heart to understanding.

____ Proverbs 2:2   d. Be mature in your understanding.

____ Proverbs 4:5   e. The breath of the Almighty gives understanding.

____ Proverbs 16:16   f. He who keeps understanding will find good.

____ Proverbs 16:22   g. May the eyes of your understanding be enlightened.

____ Proverbs 19:8   h. Give me understanding so I can keep Your law.

____ 1 Corinthians 14:20   i. Get wisdom! Get understanding!

____ Ephesians 1:18   j. Understanding is a wellspring of life.

*S*o are reading and studying one in the same? No. It's true that we need to slow down, and read for comprehension when we pick up our Bibles. But studying that Bible is something else again.

2. What term does John 5:39 use for a careful studying of the Scriptures? And what does Jesus say can be discovered by this investigation?

*A*t this time in history, the Scriptures consisted of what we now call the Old Testament. When Luke refers to *Moses*, he's talking about the first five books of the Bible, often referred to as the Pentateuch. And when he says *the Prophets*, he's referring to the Major and Minor Prophets in the Old Testament, like Isaiah, Hosea, and Zechariah. The other section of the Old Testament was the *Books of Wisdom*, which included Job, Psalms, Proverbs, Ecclesiastes, and Song of Solomon. According to Luke, these Old Testament Scriptures spoke of Jesus!

DID YOU NOTICE?

John 5:39 has a cross-reference in my Bible—Luke 24:27. "And beginning at Moses and all the Prophets, He expounded to them in all the Scriptures the things concerning Himself" (NKJV).

3. John tells us that the Scriptures are a source of eternal life because they testify of Jesus. According to Romans 10:17, what else do we as believers have because of our Bibles?

After years of reading through the Scriptures, we begin to have favorite sections. These passages become quite familiar to us, and we can say sections of them from memory. They have a lilt to them, a cadence not unlike poetry. The well-known words are like old friends. Truly, these are "beautiful words, wonderful words, wonderful words of life." But we need to stop and consider that these beautiful words are also meaningful words.

It's like going back to your hometown and finding much of it unchanged. There's the old grocery, the drug store, the used bookstore. You recognize the bank, the post office, and the school. You know every street sign, every park bench, every inch of the architecture. Main Street is your old stomping ground. But even though you can navigate the streets and even give directions to strangers, you've never actually been inside any of the shops. You know them because you used to walk by them every day. You've a kind of nodding acquaintance with each. But you've never actually stopped at the door, stepped inside, and explored these establishments for yourself.

Reading is walking the old familiar paths through the Scriptures. We understand what we read, and can navigate our way through the pages with ease. But studying means stopping in one spot, going in to explore, and unpacking the delights that can be found within. Both are needful in the life of every believer!

4. Get your Bibles open and read Acts 17:10–12. Paul is in the midst of his second missionary trip, and after a rough time in Thessalonica, is delighted with his reception in the city of Berea. How are the people of this city described?

*I*n order to read through the Bible in a year, we must get through three or four pages in our Bibles every day. But if our intent is study, four pages is too much to tackle. Four chapters, four paragraphs, even four pages can be too much. If you have the right tools, four words can take up your whole study time! Let's take a look at just four words from Acts 17:11.

5. Fair-minded. Literally, "noble," is only used four times in the New Testament. Break out your concordance and find those four passages. What can you glean about the meaning of noble by putting these four verses side by side?

6. You cannot expect to find a precious nugget of information if you don't do a good deal of digging first. Have patience as you scour your resources for tidbits of information. With some effort, you may uncover something you'll treasure! The Bereans, "received the word." What can you make of the word "received"?

*I*f you are having some trouble finding any information about these terms in the resources you have on hand, why not begin with the definitions from an ordinary dictionary? That, at least, will give you insight into the word chosen by the translators. Every little bit can help your understanding along!

7. And the word they received "with all readiness." Study and see what you can discover about "readiness."

8. Lastly, search through your various tools of the trade, and see what you can uncover about the word "searched."

DIGGING DEEPER

If the prospect of studying the original languages of the Bible leaves you shrugging your shoulders and saying, "It's all Greek to me!" don't despair. This is where *Vine's Expository Dictionary* comes in handy. It will assist you in doing word studies of Greek terms. And, if you find it too daunting a task to wade through *Vine's* definitions, turn to a trusted commentary. Most commentators take the time to explain the nuances of the words you're wondering about.

PONDER & PRAY

This week, you might like to pray for concentration. When we're attempting to study the Bible, we like to give our whole minds to the task. Interruptions and distractions are inevitable, but the Lord can help us maintain our train of thought. Also, ponder over the description of the Berean church that you've been studying. What about them did Paul find so commendable, and what can we learn from their example?

TRINKETS TO TREASURE

Have you been spending all your time on Main Street without taking the time to step into the shops to explore? Your trinket today is a snail's shell, to help remind you that studying means slowing down from the normal pace of our reading. In Bible study, our goal is not distance, but discernment. So we take the time to consider each word and phrase, poking around in our reference works to see what we can discover.

NOTES & PRAYER REQUESTS

CHAPTER FOUR

We Have a Teacher

"He opened their understanding, that they might comprehend the Scriptures."

Luke 24:45 NKJV

I n the online community, there are certain protocols that should be followed. These common courtesies constitute good online manners. You don't type your messages in all capital letters, because that would be shouting. You don't ask other people for personal information, because that would be suspicious. And you don't ask any questions until you've read the FAQs—frequently asked questions. Generally speaking, someone who is new to an online community has more enthusiasm than courtesy. They'll overwhelm a talk list with silly questions and inane chatter, much to the annoyance of more established members. It's considered bad form to post something for everyone to read if you haven't taken the time to read back through archived messages to see if the topic has already been discussed in recent history. Experienced folk have little patience for these newbies, forgetting that they were once new to these things as well.

When it comes to Bible study, many of us are

Clearing ⚐ the ⚐ Cobwebs

When you need advice, or just to talk something through, who is the person you most trust and most often turn to?

newbies. We wouldn't know a homiletic from a hermeneutic if it walked up and introduced itself. More experienced folk bandy about words like doctrinal, theological, and ontological—but we don't have a clue what they mean! They start in about original languages and majority texts, and our eyes glaze over. We don't dare ask a question, and we're not sure where the FAQs might be located. So we back away, duck out of the room, and throw in the towel over this whole Bible study thing.

> I know that I need to partake of the Living Water all day long.
> Sheila Walsh

1. Within the body of Christ, there are those who could be called newbies. What does Paul call those who are new in the faith in 1 Corinthians 3:1–2?

2. Of course, there's nothing wrong in and of itself, with being new in Christ. Paul is often quite gentle with young Christians, calling them his children. What is needed for new believers to grow, according to 1 Peter 2:2?

> For though by this time you ought to be teachers, you need someone to teach you again the first principles of the oracles of God; and you have come to need milk and not solid food. For everyone who partakes only of milk is unskilled in the word of righteousness, for he is a babe. But solid food belongs to those who are of full age, that is, those who by reason of use have their senses exercised to discern both good and evil.
>
> Hebrews 5:13–14 NKJV

3. What does Hebrews 5:12–14 have to say about newbies?

When you're not quite sure what a passage means, or if you'd like to get someone else's insights on a certain verse, you can turn to commentaries for help. A commentary is a book that comments on the Scripture, and it's a good idea to remember that these comments reflect different individuals' viewpoints and opinions. Commentaries are not infallible, but they can be invaluable resources.

A good place to start is a one-volume commentary. These cover the basics. As you get into greater depth of study, you might consider purchasing a commentary or two for the particular book of the Bible you are studying. Comparing their entries will give you a wider scope of the possible interpretations and meanings you are hunting for. Take a look at this excerpt from *Nelson's New Illustrated Bible Commentary* for Hebrews 5:12–14:

> **5:12 By this time you ought to be teachers** suggests all believers ought to be teachers not in the formal sense, but in the sense that those who have been taught ought to impart to others what they have learned through the gifts God has given them. **First principles** are basic truths. The phrase refers to the letters of the alphabet in writing or to addition and subtraction tables in arithmetic. First principles are the elements out of which everything else develops. **Have come to need:** They have retrogressed because of disuse. If you don't practice what you see and hear, you lose it and have to be told it again and again. To not use it is to loose it. **Milk . . . solid food:** The author illustrates the ingredients of growth. Milk equals input. Solid food equals output. We start with the input of truth, exercising the principle of readiness for learning. We gradually implement the principle of practice for retention of truth. Consistent and persistent practice of truth results in growth to maturity.

5:13 unskilled in the word of righteousness: The readers of this letter did not necessarily lack information concerning righteousness; they lacked experience in practicing the information they had. Maturity comes from practice. As we practice righteousness, we will have less difficulty in determining good from evil. **Babe** is a description of the spiritually immature. Babies have little discernment or self-discipline. They must constantly be told "no." Mature believers are able to know right from wrong and to control their sinful appetites.

5:14 Full age describes the spiritually mature. **Reason of use** means "practice" or "habit." Those who make a habit of obeying the message of righteousness mature in the faith and are able to distinguish good and evil.

Reading a commentary alongside our Bibles is an excellent way to facilitate study. Often times, a good study Bible will have these kinds of notes at the bottom of every page, thereby placing the commentary alongside the text. In fact, these same study notes from the *Nelson's New Illustrated Bible Commentary* can be found in the NKJV Study Bible

4. Books are very useful tools, but there are times when we wish we had someone to interact with. Often, what we want more than anything is for someone to patiently explain things to us. Strangely enough, we have a Teacher closer at hand than you think! What does Paul remind us in 1 Corinthians 6:19?

5. When Jesus left to return to His Father in heaven, He sent the Holy Spirit to live with all believers. This was foretold in Old Testament Scriptures, and explained in New Testament ones. Match these up:

___ Proverbs 1:23	a. I will pray to the Father to send you another Helper.
___ Isaiah 11:2	b. When the Helper comes, He will testify of Me.
___ Isaiah 40:13, 14	c. Have an ear to hear what the Spirit says.
___ John 14:16	d. The Spirit of the Lord shall rest upon Him.
___ John 14:17	e. You do not need anyone to teach you.
___ John 15:26	f. The Spirit searches the deep things of God.
___ 1 Corinthians 2:9, 10	g. I will pour out my spirit on you.
___ 1 Corinthians 2:13	h. The Spirit of Truth dwells with you and in you.
___ 1 John 2:27	i. The Holy Spirit teaches spiritual things.
___ Revelation 2:29	j. Who can teach the Spirit of the Lord? No one.

6. What did Jesus say that the Holy Spirit would be able to do, according to John 14:26?

7. What does John 16:13, 14 tell us the Spirit will do on our behalf?

8. The Spirit guides us into the truth. And well He should be able to! What does 2 Peter 1:21 tell us about the Scriptures we study?

9. David said, "The Spirit of the Lord spoke by me, and His word was on my tongue" (2 Sam. 23:2 NKJV). All of Scripture is Spirit-inspired. What do we learn about the Word of God from 2 Timothy 3:16–17?

DIGGING DEEPER

When asked what book, besides his Bible, he would want to have with him if he was stranded on a desert island, evangelist Billy Graham answered, "my topical Bible." When it comes to Bible Study, a topical Bible really is a godsend. It helps you to pull together verses from throughout the Bible on every major subject addressed in Scripture. One excellent topical Bible is *The MacArthur Topical Bible.*

Ponder & Pray

Have you ever considered just what the Holy Spirit, whose temple you are, does all day inside? Give that some thought this week. In fact, if you have access to a topical Bible, ponder and pray your way through the verses listed there about the Holy Spirit! This is a good week to give thanks to God that you have such a Teacher. Rejoice that you have such help in your studies.

Trinkets to Treasure

Since the focus of this lesson has been on the Holy Spirit's role in our hearts and our lives, especially as our Teacher, our trinket this week is an apple. An apple for the Teacher. When you're feeling overwhelmed by all the things you don't know, just remember that God hasn't left you to struggle through life alone. You have the Spirit, and His name is Helper. He is always with you, and will guide you into the truth.

NOTES & PRAYER REQUESTS

CHAPTER FIVE

DARE TO COMPARE

"FOR WHATEVER THINGS WERE WRITTEN BEFORE WERE WRITTEN FOR OUR LEARNING, THAT WE THROUGH THE PATIENCE AND COMFORT OF THE SCRIPTURES MIGHT HAVE HOPE."

Romans 15:4 NKJV

William Shakespeare is one of the most quotable men in all of history. In fact, he's second only to Scripture in the frequency with which he appears in footnotes. But most folks don't just pick up Shakespeare for some light afternoon reading. His plots are brilliant, but his English is truly old-style, and it takes a while to catch the meaning of his words. It helps to actually see his plays, for then the drama unfolds more naturally, with gestures and inflections helping things along.

But over the centuries, people have made small adjustments to make Shakespeare more accessible to the masses. One trick is to change the time in which the story is set. Though the wording remains the same, the look of the whole play is transformed. They've set *Much Ado About Nothing* in the Roaring 20's, and also in the 1950's, with Sinatra music to boot. I attended a production of *Henry II* in which the armies of the enemy

CLEARING ↗ THE ↖ COBWEBS

Have you ever been to the theater, or to a college or high school play? What did you see, and what did you think of it?

troops were dressed as bikers in leather and chains. Another technique used by filmmakers is to take the plot of a Shakespearean play and completely revamp it for modern audiences. This can render dear William's work almost unrecognizable. For instance, *The Taming of the Shrew* has been made over into a musical called *Kiss Me Kate*, a teen movie called *10 Things I Hate About You*, and an amusing episode of *Moonlighting*.

Now, the King James Version of the Bible was written in 1611, and many of us grew up with this translation. Still, we have to admit the English is truly old-style. We'd be hard-put to define some of the words we run across in it. So, over the years, people have tried making small adjustments in order to make it more accessible to the masses. In some cases, it's just a matter of updating a few of the words—taking out the "thee's" and "thou's." In others, the work is rewritten to such an extent, the final result is almost unrecognizable from the original. Either way, the intent is to make the Scriptures easier to understand.

*I*f digging out the Greek and Hebrew meanings of words is just a little more than you ever wanted to know, consider the value in comparing two or three translations when you're studying a verse!

Let's do a comparison of various translations for 1 Peter 1:23:

"Having been born again, not of corruptible seed but incorruptible, through the word of God which lives and abides forever"
(NKJV).

NLT	NCV	MSG
For you have been born again. Your new life did not come from your earthly parents because the life they gave you will end in death. But this new life will last forever because it comes from the eternal, living word of God.	You have been born again, and this new life did not come from something that dies, but from something that cannot die. You were born again through God's living message that continues forever.	Your new life is not like your old life. Your old birth came from mortal sperm; your new birth comes from God's living Word. Just think: a life conceived by God himself!

Here we have four different versions of the Bible. This is an excellent opportunity to break out a package of colored pencils. Starting with the *New King James Version*, we can color-code our comparison!

1. Choose a colored pencil, and shade in the phrase "Having been born again" in the *New King James Version* of 1 Peter 1:23. Now, taking the other translations one at a time, shade in the corresponding phrases with that same color. What is the variation in the wording?

2. Choose another color and begin with the phrase "not of corruptible seed." Do the paraphrases help you to understand what Peter meant by this?

3. Select a new color and shade in the phrase "but incorruptible" and its equivalent in all four versions.

4. Another color and another phrase: "through the word of God." How is this rendered in the various translations?

5. And last but not least, the final phrase "which lives and abides forever." Use yet another colored pencil to shade in the different versions of this.

6. Sometimes all it takes to make the light bulb go on for someone is to hear something explained in other words. Did comparing these four translations help you to understand this verse from 1 Peter with more clarity?

*T*here are a lot of versions of the Bible available to us. We know they're all different, because the wording varies from one to the next. Have you ever wondered what the difference is? Let's take a little time to explain what sets them apart.

First of all, some versions of the Bible are translations, or what is called a formal equivalent. These Bibles were created by going back to the original languages—Hebrew and Greek—and translating them into English, word for word. This process makes the translation incredibly accurate. Some of the most popular word-for-word versions are the *King James Version*, the *New King James Version*, and the *New American Standard Bible*.

The rest of our Bible versions are paraphrases, or what is called a dynamic equivalent. These Bibles were created, not in a word-for-word fashion, but in a thought-for-thought fashion. This means that the Bible isn't first translated, but interpreted, and rewritten in modern language. This makes these versions of the Bible quite readable. Some of the most popular thought-for-thought paraphrases of the Bible are the *New International Version*, *The Living Bible*, the *New Century Version*, *Phillip's Translation*, and *The Message*.

Two other versions of the Bible that are available don't quite fit into these two categories. One is the *New Living Translation*. This is a revision of *The Living Bible*. It is based on the original paraphrase, but the editors tweaked it so that it would be more accurate. This makes it something of a hybrid, in between a translation and a paraphrase. The other unique version is *The Amplified Bible*. This version is basically the *King James Version* of the Bible that has been supplemented—amplified—with the addition of descriptive words in brackets. These help to flesh out the color and sense of key words.

Let's turn you loose on some other passages. Each of these tells us something about God's Word. Their message may become clearer to you if you compare the wording in several different versions. Make notes of your findings, especially in cases where the wording in one translation helped you to understand the *New King James Version* more clearly. Dig in!

"But what does it say? 'The word is near you, in your mouth and in your heart' (that is, the word of faith which we preach)."
—Romans 10:8 NKJV

"For whatever things were written before were written for our learning, that we through the patience and comfort of the Scriptures might have hope."
—Romans 15:4 NKJV

"Finally, brethren, pray for us, that the word of the Lord may run swiftly and be glorified, just as it is with you."
—2 Thessalonians 3:1 NKJV

"Holding fast the word of life, so that I may rejoice in the day of Christ that I have not run in vain or labored in vain."
—Philippians 2:16 NKJV

DIGGING DEEPER

Do you spend a lot of time in the car, taking walks, folding laundry? Audio Bibles may just be the resource for you! The whole Bible is available on cassette or compact disk in a variety of translations. For the purpose of reading Scripture, these tapes allow us to really blitz through the Bible. Just one side of a tape each day gets you through the whole thing in just under three months! For study purposes, you can make a private recording of a portion— say the Book of 1 John—that you want to concentrate on. Then you can listen to that section over and over again, familiarizing yourself with it. Or, if you like comparing translations, sit down with Bible and pencil in hand—listening to one version of the Bible while following along in another!

PONDER & PRAY

Thank the Lord this week for the variety of Bible translations available to you. Each has its place. Each meets a need. We are so accustomed to having a Bible readily available that we forget it wasn't so long ago that only the priests and monks and the most learned men had access to the Scriptures, for they were only printed in Greek, Hebrew, or Latin. The uneducated, common folk could not search the Scriptures for themselves as the Berean church did!

TRINKETS TO TREASURE

Just as Shakespeare's *The Taming of the Shrew* was transformed for modern audiences into a teen movie, a television drama, and a musical, our Bible has been altered to suit today's readers. Your small token of this alteration is a shrew! This little mousy creature is a reminder that a comparison of different versions of the Bible can shed some light on difficult wording or uncertain meaning.

NOTES & PRAYER REQUESTS

CHAPTER SIX

PITFALLS

"NOT WALKING IN CRAFTINESS NOR HANDLING THE WORD OF GOD DECEITFULLY"

2 Corinthians 4:2 NKJV

W hen my daughter was just starting school, we were learning about Pocahontas, the young Indian girl who saved the life of John Smith. We progressed nicely through dates and places and tribal culture, but we came up short when I showed my little girl a portrait of Pocahontas. "No. That's not what Pocahontas looks like." I explained to her that at that time in history there were no cameras, and so all we had to go by was this formal portrait that had been painted of Pocahontas while she was in England. Though she's wearing English clothing, it was indeed Pocahontas. "No!" Adamant, and actually crying, my daughter ran to the shelves where we keep some videos, and brought back Disney's Pocahontas. "*This* is Pocahontas!" Ah. And I understood. Who would want this pale, plain girl in stiff old-fashioned hat and ruff when

CLEARING ↗ THE ↖ COBWEBS

What movies have you seen that are based on biblical events? Have you ever gone back to the Bible to see if their account matched that of Scripture?

you could choose to believe instead in a long-legged woman in short buck-skins with an independent self-assurance and the voice of an angel?

What does this have to do with Bible study? Did you know that Moses didn't really look like Charlton Heston? Seriously, we run into a whole lot of trouble in Bible study if we trade the plain truth for something that appeals to us more. For instance, let's say you have a pet notion and you'd like to prove that it's biblical, so you hunt through the Bible, pick a few likely sounding verses right out of context, and build your case on them. That little pitfall is called prooftexting. Or let's say you're reading through one of the narratives (story format), and you use your "sanctified imag-ination" to put yourselves in the shoes of the ones you're reading about. How would you have reacted? What would you have thought? And so you interpret that story based on your own feelings.

Strictly speaking, the Bible doesn't tell us what people were think-ing or feeling. We must be careful even putting our own inflections and emphasis into the words on the page. This is where Bible study needs a touch of the scholar to be accurate. Don't read your own emotions into the text. Stick to the facts, ma'am.

1. In Numbers 22:18 and 24:13, what was offered to Balaam if he would just change the word of the Lord to suit the plans of men?

2. What can stand in the way of God's Word and its effectiveness, according to Mark 7:13?

3. What did Paul find it necessary to defend himself against in 2 Corinthians 2:17?

4. What does Paul say he would never do in 2 Corinthians 4:2?

DID YOU NOTICE?

The cross-reference printed after 2 Corinthians 2:17 points us to 2 Peter 2:3. In this passage, Peter warns the church of the dangers of false teaching.

But there were also false prophets among the people, even as there will be false teachers among you, who will secretly bring in destructive heresies, even denying the Lord who bought them, and bring on themselves swift destruction. And many will follow their destructive ways, because of whom the way of truth will be blasphemed. By covetousness they will exploit you with deceptive words; for a long time their judgment has not been idle, and their destruction does not slumber.

2 Peter 2:1–3 NKJV

Read through this passage slowly, highlighting all of the negative words used to describe the false teachers.

*A*nother pitfall is picking and choosing which Bible truths you'll believe. You can't welcome those parts you're most comfortable with and ignore the ones you'd rather not believe. We're talking about God's Word here, not a smorgasbord!

5. Now take a look at 2 Peter 3:16. In this verse, Peter is talking about Paul's writings. What danger does this verse warn about?

6. Check out your study notes or a commentary on 2 Peter 3:15–16. What interesting tidbit does this verse reveal about Paul's writings?

7. There's a very good reason why seminarians go through years of training in biblical interpretation. When do mistakes happen, according to Matthew 22:29?

8. Take a look at 2 Peter 1:20. What would you think this verse means? Now take a look at study notes and commentaries. Does your understanding of this verse change slightly?

*I*f there's one pitfall I want for you to avoid, it's getting too big for your britches. Guard against pride in your ability to "rightly divide the Word of truth." You definitely don't know enough until you know that you don't know it all.

9. We need to treat the Word of God with care and respect. No twisting, tampering, or tweaking is allowed. We can't spin it in our favor or put a slant on it. God says His Word is what it is, and no messing around will be tolerated. What do each of these passages warn?

- Deuteronomy 4:2

- Deuteronomy 12:32

- Revelation 22:18, 19

DIGGING DEEPER

Journals are a wonderful place to interact with the Scriptures you are studying. You can make lists of synonyms for key words, put two translations of a verse side by side, chase cross-references throughout the Bible, and collect all those sticky-note inspirations and inquiries in one place. Journals become our collections of thoughts and prayers. They help us to work through our understanding of Bible verses and how they apply to us personally.

PONDER & PRAY

This week, pray for a healthy dose of respect, humility, and integrity when it comes to handling the Scriptures. We don't know everything, but we can learn if we are teachable. There will always be those who twist the truth, whether intentionally or out of ignorance. This week's lesson reminds us that we must be careful in our own interpretation of the Bible, and also to be discerning as we listen to the teaching of others.

TRINKETS TO TREASURE

Your trinket this week is a mousetrap which shall serve to remind you of the various traps, snares, and pitfalls that can surround biblical interpretation. God's Word is His own, and He will not stand for those who add their own injunctions, subtract the bits they don't feel comfortable with, bend the truth to suit their situation, or twist its meaning altogether. The truth of the Bible can stand on its own, and we are wise when we stand upon it.

NOTES & PRAYER REQUESTS

CHAPTER SEVEN

BACK TO THE BASICS

"OPEN MY EYES THAT I MAY SEE WONDROUS THINGS FROM YOUR LAW."

Psalm 119:18 NKJV

God has gifted some individuals with great curiosity. For instance, my son is very curious about how things fit together and how they work. When he was two, he could pick the lock on our bedroom door. (I'm not kidding!) He enjoys nothing more than taking things apart, figuring out how they work, and putting them back together again. He's disassembled ballpoint pens, unscrewed switch plates, and swapped the lines on our phone jacks. I expect this fascination will escalate until he does something like what my uncle did—take apart an entire motorcycle, carefully laying out each piece on oil-stained tarps, then reassembling it. Is this just a guy thing?

So how does this relate to Bible study? Well, it's all in the pieces and parts. We're not talking about literal nuts and bolts here, but figurative

CLEARING ↗ THE ↖ COBWEBS

Set your mind to it for a few minutes, and consider—how many different parts of speech can you name?

The promises of God and the power of this Spirit are mine to rely upon without ever waiting.
Luci Swindoll

ones. Much of careful Bible study comes down to taking the sentences in our Bible apart, understanding every little nuance of these parts, then reassembling them with a better understanding of how they work. We're talking about getting back to the basics here—grammar! Parts of speech. Nouns. Pronouns. Modifiers. Verbs and verb tenses. Word order. If we can figure out how all these small parts fit together, we can understand the whole with confidence.

1. Let's do a little review of our grammar together, shall we? "Is" is a being verb, and it equates two things. If we say "God is love," we could just as easily say "God = love." Look at these verses. What do they tell us about the Word of God?

"Every word of God is _____."—Proverbs 30:5 NKJV

"The word of the Lord is _____."—Psalm 18:30 NKJV

"For the word of the Lord is _____."—Psalm 33:4 NKJV

2. Now lets look at some verbs. These verses also tell us something about God's Word. Highlight the verb in each of these verses that tells us what the Word does.

"I have written to you, fathers, because you have known Him who is from the beginning. I have written to you, young men, because you are strong, and the word of God abides in you, And you have overcome the wicked one."
—1 John 2:14 NKJV

"For this reason we also thank God without ceasing, because when you received the word of God which you heard from us, you welcomed it not as the word of men, but as it is in truth, the word of God, which effectively works in you who believe."
—1 Thessalonians 2:13 NKJV

"But the word of the Lord endures forever. Now this is the word which by the gospel was preached to you."—1 Peter 1:25 NKJV

3. Sometimes we can learn just as much from what the Bible tells us a thing *is* as we can from what it tells us it *isn't*. What do these verses tell us that the Word of God is not?

• John 10:35

> *Sometimes I have more questions than answers, and maybe that's part of faith.*
>
> Patsy Clairmont

• 2 Timothy 2:9

*W*hen we're studying our Bibles, we need to slow down a bit, and start noticing how the words and sentences work together. What details can we pick up? What verbs jump out at us?

4. What can we do with the Word of God? How do we respond to it?

Acts 4:4—"Many of those who heard the word _____"
(NKJV).

Acts 4:31—"They were filled with the Holy Spirit, and they _____ the word of God with _____" (NKJV).

Acts 13:48—"They were _____ and _____ the word of the Lord" (NKJV).

Hebrews 6:5—"Have _____ the good word of God" (NKJV).

*A*nother useful technique for breaking down large sections into smaller pieces is to read through a passage more than once, each time looking for certain things. Let's take a look at a portion of Psalm 119, the longest chapter in all of Scripture. This whole psalm is a poem, broken down into sections based on the letters of the Hebrew alphabet, which praises God's Word. We'll just take on the first twenty-four verses for today's exercise.

Blessed are the undefiled in the
way,
Who walk in the law of the Lord!
Blessed are those who keep His
testimonies,
Who Seek Him with the whole
heart!
They also do no iniquity;
The walk in His ways.
You have commanded us
To keep Your precepts diligently.
Oh, that my ways were directed
To keep Your statutes!
Then I would not be ashamed,
When I look into all Your
commandments.
I will praise You with uprightness
of heart,
When I learn Your righteous
judgments.
I will keep Your statutes;
Oh, do not forsake me utterly!

How can a young man cleanse his
way?
By taking heed according to Your
word.
With my whole heart I have
sought You;
Oh, let me not wander from Your
commandments!
Your word I have hidden in my
heart,
That I might not sin against You.
Blessed are You, O Lord!
Teach me Your statutes.

With my lips I have declared
All the judgments of Your mouth.
I have rejoiced in the way of Your
testimonies,
As much as in all riches.
I will meditate on Your precepts,
And contemplate Your ways.
I will delight myself in Your
statutes;
I will not forget Your word.

Deal bountifully with Your
servant,
That I may live and keep Your
word.
Open my eyes, that I may see
Wondrous things from Your law.
I am a stranger in the earth;
Do not hide Your commandments
from me.
My soul breaks with longing
For Your judgments at all times.
You rebuke the proud—the
cursed,
Who stray from Your
commandments.
Remove from me reproach and
contempt,
For I have kept Your testimonies.
Princes also sit and speak against
me,
But Your servant meditates on
Your statutes.
Your testimonies also are my
delight
And my counselors.

5. With a blue highlighter or colored pencil, shade in all the words that describe the things which are right to do—our good actions and attitudes—according to Psalm 119:1–24.

6. Now take an orange highlighter or colored pencil, and shade in all the words that describe the actions and attitudes we do not want to exhibit, as we find them in Psalm 119:1–24.

7. Read through the passage again, this time looking for the things that God does for those who love Him. Use a purple highlighter or colored pencil for these instances.

8. Now, with a green highlighter or colored pencil in hand, read through the passage one more time, this time shading in the descriptions of what God can do to those who resist Him.

9. Last of all, with a yellow highlighter or colored pencil, go through and shade all the mentions of God's Word in this passage. With the exception of a handful, every verse in Psalm 119 refers to Scripture by its many synonyms. What are they here?

DIGGING DEEPER

If you enjoy this kind of study—looking for the verbs or adjectives within sentences—I'd like to suggest a project that could keep you busy for years. As you read through the Scriptures, keep an eye out for verbs specifically used with God—the things He does. Pick a special colored pencil or highlighter, and use it to mark each action. If you started in Genesis 1, you'd have "God creates," "God speaks," "God sees," "God divides," and "God names" all in the first five verses! What better way to get to know our Lord than by studying Him!

PONDER & PRAY

In Psalm 119, the psalmist praised God's Word and prayed for a wholehearted passion for it. See what he desires? To seek it, learn it, walk in it, hide it in his heart, treasure it more than riches, meditate on it, contemplate it, seek its counsel, and delight in it! What singular devotion! What earnest longings! This week, make the psalmist's prayers your own prayers. Ask the Lord to open your eyes and teach you the joys of desiring His Word.

TRINKETS TO TREASURE

Since getting down to the nuts and bolts of Bible study can be much like taking apart the nuts and bolts of an engine, your trinket for the week will be a nut and bolt. In order to understand how the words in a sentence work together, we have to take them apart, look them over one at a time. Then, when we've put them back together again, we have a much clearer understanding of how each piece fits in with those around them. In Bible study, our nuts and bolts are nouns and verbs, adjectives and adverbs.

Notes & Prayer Requests

CHAPTER EIGHT

OUTLINES

"IT SEEMED GOOD TO ME . . .
TO WRITE YOU AN ORDERLY ACCOUNT."

Luke 1:3 NKJV

Quilting is one of my various hobbies. There are shelves of fabric in our spare bedroom, all arranged according to color. I've made doll quilts, baby quilts, wall quilts and bed quilts. One of the things I love most about quilting is choosing the next quilt pattern I'll make. All the patterns have such wonderful names—Dresden Plate, Tennessee Waltz, Snail's Trail, Tumbling Blocks, Puss in the Corner, Lover's Knot, Broken Dishes, Northern Winds, Wild Goose Chase, Double Wedding Ring. One of my favorites is a quilt now draped across the back of the couch in the family room at my folk's house. I gave it to my Mom a few years back as a gift. The pattern is called Corn and Beans. At first, all you see is a riot of colors in an Americana color scheme—navy blue, barn red, warm gold, soft browns. At a glance, there's no apparent pattern, just a jumble of triangles in different sizes. You'll notice that one

CLEARING THE COBWEBS

When you know you've got a big trip coming up, and you're giddy with anticipation over it, how soon ahead of time do you begin working on a packing list?

67

triangle has chickens scattered across it. One is deep blue with tiny white stars. Another has tiny words closely written, which on closer inspection prove to say, "moo moo moo moo moo." These are fleeting impressions, and don't help you see the big picture. But if you lay the quilt out on the floor and study it for a couple of minutes, the design becomes apparent.

Many times we'll be reading through a chapter in our Bibles, and we'll have to admit to ourselves that while we feel the truth of what we've read, we're really only latching on to a phrase here and there. It's as if we're picking out a haphazard triangle along the quilt top, and enjoying its color and texture, but we've no idea how it fits in with the triangles around it. We can't see the design. That's where outlines can help us. They help us sort through all those words on the page by spreading them out so we can study their pattern. A good study Bible will give you an outline of each book of the Bible as you come to it. Some will even go so far as to outline each chapter. We can use outlines to understand the writer's design, and see how the "triangles" that catch our attention fit into the larger pattern.

> *It's amazing to me how God knows our every desire, even unexpressed or unconscious.*
> Thelma Wells

1. What does Paul urge us to hold on to in 2 Timothy 1:13?

2. What can you find out about this "pattern of sound words" in your various research tools?

> *Hold fast the pattern of sound words which you have heard from me,*
> *in faith and love which are in Christ Jesus.*
> 2 Timothy 1:13 NKJV

*O*utlines are excellent study tools. An outline plots the logical progress of any lecture, sermon, or book of the Bible. Breaking the flow of words into points and sub-points helps us to recall the whole more easily afterwards. In Bible study, outlines are invaluable. They help us to divine the main points of a paragraph, to follow the author's line of thinking, to distinguish the main point from its related sub-points. You understand a passage of Scripture when you are able to outline it

3. Let's start small by outlining these three verses from Ephesians 5—which mention the action of the Word in a believer's life:

> *"Christ . . . loved the church and gave Himself for it, that He might sanctify and cleanse it with the washing of water by the word, that He might present it to Himself a glorious church, not having spot or wrinkle or any such thing, but that it should be holy and without blemish."*
> —Ephesians 5:25–27 NKJV

4. Let's do another. This time, tackle Hebrews 1:1–3, which again mentions the working of the word within its context:

> *"God, who at various times and in different ways spoke in time past to the fathers by the prophets, has in these last days spoken to us by His Son, whom He has appointed heir of all things, through whom also He made the worlds; who being the brightness of His glory and the express image of His person, and upholding all things by the word of His power, when He had by Himself purged our sins, sat down at the right hand of the Majesty on high."*
> —Hebrews 1:1–3 NKJV

When you're outlining, you don't have to go back to the old system of Roman numerals and capital letters if you don't want to. Just take the section verb by verb, phrase by phrase. Keep main points on the outside edge, and indent the sub-points under them. This should be enough to chart out the flow of thoughts.

5. Here is a section that speaks of the Word of God and its role in creation. Outline it as well:

"For this they willfully forget: that by the word of God the heavens were of old, and the earth standing out of the water and in the water by which the world that then existed perished, being flooded with water. But the heavens and the earth which now exist are kept in store by the same word, reserved for fire until the day of judgment and perdition of ungodly men."

—2 Peter 3:5–7 NKJV

6. Let's take a quick side-trip from our outlines to address a couple of questions about the Word and its place in the creation of all things. What does Psalm 33:6 have to say on the subject?

> *By faith we understand that the worlds were framed by the word of God, so that the things which are seen were not made of things which are visible.*
> Hebrews 11:3 NKJV

7. What does Hebrews 11:3 say that we take by faith?

8. One more outline for today. Take a careful look the Parable of the Sower, found in Luke 8:4–15. Don't worry about outlining every word. Read through it a couple of times, then outline the main points. And as you work, keep in mind what you are learning about the Word of God and its work in our hearts.

Closely related to the technique of outlining is that of list-making. Are you a list-maker? Many of us have a secret passion for lists—grocery lists, to-do lists, wish lists, honey-do lists, packing lists. We create lists of goals, resolutions, and books we intend to read someday. Lists of friends we owe thank you notes to, errands we need to run this afternoon, things we want to achieve before we're 40, 50, 60, 70! Why, we're so attached to our lists, if we've gone and done something that *isn't* on our list, we'll add it just to have the satisfaction of crossing it off! Those of you who love listing, you'll be delighted to know that lists are yet another tool of Bible study.

9. One way of making lists is to look at a passage of Scripture and list what you find there. Let's turn again to Psalm 119, this time to verses 97–104. Create a list, based on this passage, of all the statements made about the Word of God. Would you want this list to be your own list as well?

> When we study faith in the biblical context, it has both an active and a passive sense. In an active sense, faith is our loyalty and devotion to God; in a passive sense, our resting confidence in God, in His Word, and in His promises.
> Sheila Walsh

10. Another way to make lists is to use your reference tools to your best advantage. If you have access to a Topical Bible, turn to the section on Scripture and create a list of all of the names for the Scriptures.

DIGGING DEEPER

The whole Bible has been outlined more than once! So if you like to hit the highlights, and see how all those chapters and verses work together, start hunting up resources that do the outlining for you. Many Bibles include an outline at the start of each book. Most commentaries include extensive outlines of the books they study.

PONDER & PRAY

The Bible presents us with an orderly account. God had a hand in each and every word that was chosen, and there is a clear message throughout the pages of Scripture. We come along afterwards, and try to find that pattern and glimpse that design. Pray this week for an orderly mind, able to discern the patterns of words and phrases. Ask the Lord to help you see the big picture as you study the smaller ones.

TRINKETS TO TREASURE

Whether we're in a book of Old Testament prophecy or one of Paul's New Testament epistles, there is a plan, a pattern, an outline behind the words. This week's trinket is a quilt block. In a complicated quilt pattern, we must lay it all out and study it before the pattern becomes apparent. Then, the tumble of triangles comes into focus, and we can see the design. With Scripture, laying out the writer's words and outlining them helps us to pick out the main points of a passage and to summarize its message.

Notes & Prayer Requests

CHAPTER NINE

WORD STUDIES

"LET THE WORD OF CHRIST DWELL IN YOU RICHLY IN ALL WISDOM."

Colossians 3:16 NKJV

The greeting card business seems to be a booming one. There's hardly a major holiday, event, celebration, or season of life that doesn't have its own line of cards to help mark its passing. Birthday cards, anniversary cards, sympathy cards, graduations cards. There are cards for new babies, for bon voyages, for get well soon, and for just because. Cards can say "I'm sorry," "I'm glad we're friends," "I miss you," and "Thinking of you!"

Browsing through the card section in a store can be fun. But finding just the right card for a friend can be tough. The picture on the card has to be something we know they'll love. The sentiment on the inside needs to reflect our own feelings— not too silly, not too sappy, and sure to make her smile. This may be a store-bought card, but it has to be something obviously chosen by us! By agonizing over the racks and spinners in the store, we're guaranteeing that our friends recognize our personal touch in the choosing!

CLEARING ↗ THE ↖ COBWEBS

What words were popular slang during your high school years?

> *Whatever you have learned or received or heard from me, or seen in me—put it into practice.*
>
> Philippians 4:9 NIV

When it comes to Bible study, we need to keep in mind that the Word of God is His message for us. Every word of it comes to us by His inspiration. It's His choosing, His preference, His personal touch. So when we come to study, we don't want to miss a thing, so we do well to make sure we understand every word. When we do a word study, we do two things. First, we make sure we understand exactly what is meant by a word in the verse we're studying. Second, we take a look at how that very same word is used throughout the Bible. We'll begin by making sure we understand what each of the key words in these verses mean.

"Be diligent to present yourself approved to God, a worker who does not need to be ashamed, rightly dividing the word of truth"
—2 Timothy 2:15 NKJV

1. Begin by doing a word study of the word "diligent." You might want to start with a dictionary, a Bible dictionary, and an expository dictionary.

2. Often, what we're looking for is some connotation or word color that doesn't carry over from the original language into English. What can you uncover in your resources about the phrase, "present yourself"?

3. Expository dictionaries give us "word pictures," which illustrate to us how the original recipients of these pages from our Bible would have understood them. What can you find out by doing a word study of "approved"?

> *When we take the tiniest step toward welcoming growth, he brings the fruit.*
> Luci Swindoll

4. One more term from 2 Timothy 2:15. What can you discover about the words, "rightly dividing"?

*W*ords can be tricky things. Over time they can change. Their meanings shift. They take on new significances. Slang words come in and out of style, temporarily convoluting the meanings of otherwise harmless expressions. Let me give you a couple of examples. Our first word's true definition is "causing terror or great fear." Its synonyms in the thesaurus include words like unpleasant, dreadful, frightful, monstrous, appalling, upsetting, shocking, and terrorizing. But over time, this definition has been all but forgotten. It's been replaced by a decade's old slang definition. What's the word? Terrific. Its root is the same as terror, and terrific originally referred to something that instilled terror.

Here's another one. Our second word's true definition is, "so implausible as to elicit disbelief; completely unbelievable." The synonyms in the thesaurus include words like preposterous, questionable, implausible, absurd, outlandish, unthinkable, and ridiculous. Again, we don't much think of these terms anymore when we use this term. The word? Incredible. Its root has to do with credibility, and incredible originally meant you had none!

In Bible study, make sure you're sure what each word in the verse you're studying means!

"Let the word of Christ dwell in your richly in all wisdom, teaching and admonishing one another in psalms and hymns and spiritual songs, singing with grace in your hearts to the Lord"
—Colossians 3:16 NKJV

5. Now we're going to take a look at a few words from Colossians 3:16. Begin with the word "dwell."

6. What about "richly"? What does it mean when we say, "Let the word of Christ dwell in you richly"?

7. One more for Colossians 3:16. What can you discover about "admonishing"?

> *Ah yes . . . the sweet words of the Father . . . the ultimate menu from which I want always to have my soul's palate delighted, my appetite satisfied, and my fork poised in a position of readiness.*
>
> Marilyn Meberg

8. We choose our words with care, and so does the Lord. What does Matthew 5:18 have to say about every little bit of God's Word?

9. What does Jesus mean by "jot and tittle"? Use your resources to find out.

DIGGING DEEPER

Your best tool in doing Bible word studies is your *Strong's Concordance*. With this, you can find every occurrence of one word or another in Scripture. Then, all you need to do is sift through them and see what turns up. Yes, it takes time. But the joy of discovery is worth the work.

Ponder & Pray

May your heart be filled with wonder over God's rich message for us. Even a lifetime is not long enough to grasp all that our Bibles hold. There is always something new. Our hearts always respond to its truth. Pray that the Lord will fill you with wonder over what you have access to through His Word. Pray for continued hunger to understand it.

Trinkets to Treasure

When we're out shopping for greeting cards, we're very choosy. We want to pick out one that exactly fits our needs. Your trinket this week will help to remind you that God has chosen His words carefully, and we can learn much by studying each of them. A greeting card only carries one small sentiment, but God's Word is rich in truth, prophecy, and promises. We are enriched when we study each small part of it.

Notes & Prayer Requests

CHAPTER TEN

THEMES

"MY HEART IS OVERFLOWING WITH A GOOD THEME."

Psalm 45:1 NKJV

*I*t's one of the earliest crafts we're taught in kindergarten. Taking brightly colored strips of construction paper, we weave them together. Over, under, over, under. Such a pretty pattern. As we moved on into middle school, we graduated to hand looms and yarn. Over, under, over, under. What a lovely pot holder! Weaving changes thread into fabric. The thicker the threads and the looser the weaving, the rougher the woven fabric. We're talking burlap, here. The finer the threads and tighter the weave, the more delicate the result. Silk, anyone? When colored threads are used, they create patterns in the finished fabric. Skilled craftsmen created whole scenes in their tapestries. But even the most detailed depictions, when scrutinized, turn out to be threads. Over, under, over, under. What a piece of medieval art!

Scripture is sometimes compared with woven fabric. So many authors wrote our Bible, with the

CLEARING THE COBWEBS

Do you have a theme song? If you had to choose one, what would it be?

> *Isn't God good? Isn't it amazing how, while we're in the midst of what may seem like ho-hum, ordinary, everyday routines and careers, we're actually living out pieces of the puzzle that will eventually create the big picture God has planned for our lives?*
>
> Thelma Wells

writings happening over centuries of time. Yet the finished Word is neatly woven together. Perfect, seamless, sound. We talk a lot about context when we study the Bible. When we're studying a verse, we look at its context—the surrounding material—to help us understand exactly what the phrases mean. The setting—the context—makes the author's intentions clear. Context comes from a Latin word, *contextus*, which means "to join together." The root of the Latin word for context is *textus*, which literally means, "to weave." So when we're looking at the context of a passage, we're trying to see how it has been woven in with the rest of the verses in its paragraph, its chapter, its book.

Studying Bible themes is like choosing one thread, and following it throughout the whole of Scripture. All the questions in this lesson are pulled together according to one theme that runs through the Bible. Can you figure out what that theme is? Try to summarize it by the end of the lesson!

1. What does David pray for in Psalm 143:8?

2. Jesus compared His relationship with His followers as that of a shepherd with his sheep. What does He tell us about His relationship to His sheep in John 10:3 and John 10:27?

3. Unfortunately, there is something that can stand in the way—us! What do each of these verses warn against?

Jeremiah 17:23—"But they did not _____ nor _____ their _____, but made their _____ _____, that they might not _____ nor _____ _____"
(NKJV).

Matthew 13:15—"For the _____ of this people have _____ _____. Their _____ are _____ of _____, and their _____ they have _____, lest they should _____ with their _____ and _____ with their _____, lest they should _____ with their _____ and _____" (NKJV).

Hebrews 3:15—"Today, if you will _____ His _____, do not _____ your _____ as in the _____"
(NKJV).

4. We deceive ourselves when our lives do not reflect what we say we believe. What does Ezekiel 33:31–32 say about those who live this way?

5. What does Jesus say is blessed in Matthew 13:16?

6. What does Luke 11:28 say is even more blessed?

7. Who does Romans 2:13 say is justified?

8. What does James 1:22 remind us about our responsibility as believers?

> But be doers of the word,
> and not hearers only,
> deceiving yourselves.
> James 1:22 NKJV

9. What are the blessing and warning in Revelation 1:3?

*D*id you catch the theme that is woven through all of those verses? We began with Scriptures that spoke of our desire and ability to hear God. Then, we looked at the thing that can stand in the way of our ability to hear God—our own refusal to listen! Next, we saw that those who hear are blessed, but that those who hear and obey are even more blessed. The thread that we followed was that of hearing, but we were able to draw out applications from that study. Knowing God's Word is not enough. We are called to keep it, obey it, do it!

DIGGING DEEPER

Would you like to do more study of the themes in our Scriptures? They're not difficult to find. Some themes run through the whole of the Bible. Try tracing the theme of promise, by looking at promise, promised, and the Promise. Or have some fun doing a study of numbers, by looking at how often the number twelve appears throughout Scripture. Another interesting thing to do is to hunt up themes within the writings of one man, like Paul, Luke, or John. You can explore themes within a single book, like the servanthood of Christ in Mark or the compassion of Jesus in Luke. Bible reading and Bible study become more interesting if you're looking for something as you go.

> *Sometimes we know we need refreshment but are too lazy in the routine of life—or too preoccupied with what we think is "important"—to stop for spiritual replenishment.*
>
> Sheila Walsh

PONDER & PRAY

Consider the intricacy of God's woven words this week. Throughout all these books of the Bible, written by so many different men over so many centuries, God's message is clear, consistent, changeless. Ask God to help you glimpse the threads that gleam in the fabric of the Word. Ask Him to help you follow those threads, to hear His Words, and to keep them.

TRINKETS TO TREASURE

Scripture is as intricately woven as the gorgeous tapestries of master craftsmen of old. The whole is vibrant with graceful lines and dramatic scenes, but closer inspection reveals that the whole is formed tiny threads, carefully woven into the design. Your trinket this week is a spool of thread, to remind you that when we study the Scriptures more closely, we can pick up threads that go through the whole of the Word. We can focus on that one thread, study it, and learn from our scrutiny.

Notes & Prayer Requests

CHAPTER ELEVEN

SOAKING

"MY MOUTH SHALL SPEAK WISDOM, AND THE MEDITATION OF MY HEART SHALL GIVE UNDERSTANDING."

Psalm 49:3 NKJV

When the weather is cool—late fall, winter, early spring—my crockpot is my best friend in the kitchen. Toss in a few ingredients after breakfast, and dinner will be on the table come evening. But when the days get longer and warmer, our whole menu-plan switches over into summer-mode. It's time to break out the grill! Between the savory fare we pull off the charcoal and the fresh delights provided by the farmer's market, we make the most of summer's bounty. To spice things up a little, we usually marinate our meat before putting it on the grill. A marinade is a liquid mixture in which meat or vegetables can be soaked before cooking. Usually, this concoction has oil and vinegar and a combination of herbs and spices. The seasonings penetrate the meat during the soaking process, imparting their flavor to the finished meal. All kinds of things

CLEARING ⌁ THE ⌁ COBWEBS

Summer brings with it many fresh fruits and vegetables. What's your favorite fresh summer fare?

I need intimate contact with God. Our souls were made for this. When we deprive our souls of that very life force, we can survive—but that is all we are doing. We were not created to merely survive but to thrive in God.
Sheila Walsh

can be used as ingredients in a marinade—aromatic oils, garlic, onions, fruit juices, wine vinegar, tomato paste, yogurt, sugar, soy sauce, even peanut butter! Each enhances and even improves the flavor and texture of your food. The range of possibilities keeps us experimenting with different combinations all summer long.

When it comes to Scripture, we have already talked about slowing down our pace and paying attention to each word. This is the change from reading to studying. But there's yet another downshift we need to employ, from studying to meditation. God encourages us to soak in His Words. We need to marinate ourselves in the Scriptures.

1. What does David invite the Lord to do in both Psalm 5:1 and Psalm 64:1?

2. Meditation is easiest when things are quiet. According to Psalm 77:6 and Psalm 119:148, when did the psalmist say he did some of his meditation?

3. What does Psalm 1:2 say about the timing of our meditations?

> *But his delight is in the law of the LORD, and in His law he meditates day and night.*
>
> Psalm 1:2 NKJV

4. Why is Joshua told to meditate on God's Word in Joshua 1:8?

5. Here are a bunch of different verses that talk about the things we should meditate on. Match them up:

___ Psalm 77:12   a. I will meditate on Your wondrous works.

___ Psalm 119:15   b. I muse on the work of Your hands.

___ Psalm 119:27   c. I will meditate on all Your work.

___ Psalm 119:97   d. I will meditate on His name.

___ Psalm 119:99   e. I meditate all day on the law You love.

___ Psalm 143:5   f. I will meditate on Your glorious majesty.

___ Psalm 145:5   g. I will contemplate Your ways.

___ Malachi 3:16   h. Your testimonies are my meditation.

6. According to Psalm 19:14 and Psalm 104:34, what does David want God to see in his meditations?

> *"Therefore you shall lay up these words of mine in your heart and in your soul."*
> Deuteronomy 11:18 NKJV

7. How can we know what things will be pleasing to the Lord? What does Philippians 4:8 urge us to meditate upon?

8. What does Paul tell us can be the result of a life liberally marinated in God's Word, according to 1 Timothy 4:15?

> *Each day the Lord gives us brings with it a reason to rejoice.*
> Thelma Wells

DIGGING DEEPER

This might be a good time to mention Scripture memorization. It certainly helps the meditation process to have the verse you're reflecting on committed to memory. If you want to memorize God's Word, take an intentional and systematic approach. You might use your topical Bible to pick a theme and memorize the various Scriptures related to that theme. You might choose a psalm, and commit it to memory. Or, you might tackle a whole book of the Bible.

PONDER & PRAY

This week, you can be praying for a mind attuned to pondering! Choose a passage this week and commit it to memory, then meditate on it throughout the day. Meditate, mumble, talk to yourself! Say it over, consider its meaning, contemplate its application. Spend the week soaking in the Scriptures. Marinate until it penetrates your heart and soul.

TRINKETS TO TREASURE

We marinate in oils, spices, vinegars, garlic, and herbs to impart their flavors to meat and vegetables before grilling them. By soaking meat in a marinade, the flavors are able to penetrate and lend their savor to the finished dish. This week's trinket is an indispensable marinade ingredient—garlic—to remind us that we can be marinating ourselves. When we meditate on the Scriptures, it's like soaking in God's Word. The Word penetrates our hearts and souls, imparting goodness in our lives.

CHAPTER TWELVE

WHY BOTHER?

"SEARCH FROM THE BOOK OF THE LORD, AND READ: NOT ONE OF THESE SHALL FAIL."

Isaiah 34:16 NKJV

hy do we study the Bible? Why do we fill notebooks and journals with observations and comments and questions? Is it for academic reasons—the acquisition of knowledge for its own sake? Do we want to possess knowledge? Are we accumulating knowledge like a collector does her teacups or her teddy bears? Do we have hopes of becoming champions of Bible trivia on the Quiz Bowl circuit? Do we have aspirations of becoming counselors, lecturers, authors, experts? Are we trying to impress our friends, our pastors, our Lord? Are we just zealous in our accumulation of knowledge because it's the right thing to do? Do we study our Bibles because it's the current Christian fad? Why do we bother?

Let's spend this last lesson putting Bible study in its proper place. Oh yes, our study of the Scriptures is very, very important. There's no denying that! But it is not the be all and end all of the Christian life. We study something that is

CLEARING THE COBWEBS

Are you a collector? What do you collect?

living and powerful. We grapple with eternal truths. We delve into the divine Word of God. We study God's unchanging Word so that it can change us.

1. What vital fact does 1 Corinthians 13:2 remind us of?

Though I have the _____ of _____, (If I could speak for God)

and _____ all _____ (and could unravel any enigma)

and all _____, (and knew all there was to know)

and though I have all _____, (and have perfect trust)

so that I could _____ _____, (enough to do the miraculous)

but have not _____, (but cared nothing for others)

I am _____. (I will have missed the whole point!)

2. According to Isaiah 55:11, what does God say about His purposes for His Word?

> *Belonging to Jesus Christ means that you've been given a heart transplant. With a new heart, He gives the power to be joyful, exuberant, and thankful. Eternal values replace temporary ones.*
> Barbara Johnson

God has plans. He's got purposes. And He'll accomplish what He's set out to do through His Word. So let's look at some of the things that the Word of God does in our hearts and in our lives. These are some of the reasons that we should bother to study!

3. What does John 17:17 tell us the Word is able to do in our lives?

4. What does paying attention to the Word and what it tells us accomplish in the heart according to Psalm 119:9?

5. What does Acts 20:32 tell us that God's Word is able to do in our lives?

6. What does Psalm 19:11 tell us about the role of the Word in our walk with God?

7. If this seems so far to be a whole lot of "good for you" and not enough "feel good," what promise can we glean from Psalm 19:8 and Psalm 119:111?

8. Why does Paul tell us we have these Scriptures? What reasons does he give in Romans 15:4?

DIGGING DEEPER

It's always difficult to move forward with Bible study if you don't have someone else giving you an assignment. We work best with some kind of purpose. So what can you do? Put yourself on a Scripture reading program, whether it's a through-the-Bible-in-a-year program or just a chapter a day. While you're reading, have a theme you're watching for as you go. But then, choose another section for actual study. Take it slowly, and keep a notebook or journal of your discoveries. If you're not sure where to start, why not follow along with your pastor's current sermon series, or your Sunday school lesson plan?

PONDER & PRAY

We all know we should read and study our Bibles, but there are always so many other things that intrude on our best intentions. Pray that the Lord will help you to carve out a time that you can dedicate to reading, study, and prayer. These things are your source of spiritual life and strength. Ask for the Spirit to stir up a hunger and thirst in your souls for these spiritual things.

TRINKETS TO TREASURE

One of our verses this week says that we've chosen God's Word as our heritage. It is when we do this that we find great joy. To remind us of this, our last trinket is a gold coin—treasure! Only this isn't earthly treasure that we've chosen, it's an eternal one.

NOTES & PRAYER REQUESTS

Shall We Review?

Every chapter has added a new trinket to your treasure trove of memories. Let's remind ourselves of the lessons they hold for us!

1. A Pencil.

Our Bibles are God's own words. We read them with joy, and study them with fascination. Whenever we study our Bibles, we should have a pencil in our hands.

2. A Sticky-Note.

Though perhaps one of the smallest, these handy notes are just one of the tools of the Bible study trade. When we read, we're to keep them close at hand.

3. A Snail's Shell

We need to slow down when we want to study our Bibles. Reading is always good, but in order to understand each word in each verse, we must take them one at a time.

4. An Apple

This trinket was our apple for the Teacher. The Holy Spirit abides with us as our Helper and Teacher. He helps us to understand, and guides us into the truth.

5. A Shrew

Just as Shakespeare's *The Taming of the Shrew* was remade to make it more understandable to the average person, our Bible has been translated and paraphrased so that we can read it with understanding.

6. A Mousetrap
There are pitfalls, traps, and snares surrounding Bible study. No one may add, subtract, ignore, or twist the truth. We must take care to let the Bible stand on its own.

7. A Nut and Bolt
To understand our Bibles better, we take the sentences apart, study each small piece, then put them back together again. That way, we understand how every bit works together.

8. A Quilt Block
The pattern of a complicated quilt can be hard to understand. We have to lay it out and study it if we want the design to become apparent. In Bible study, laying things out for study means outlining.

9. A Greeting Card
We're just as choosy about finding the perfect greeting card as God was in choosing His words for us. Studying the meaning of the key words in Scripture can enrich our understanding of God's message.

10. A Spool of Thread
Scripture is intricately woven together, yet we can pick out one thread and follow it through the Bible. We do this when we study a theme.

11. Garlic

A traditional marinade ingredient, this trinket reminds us that meditating on God's Word is like marinating. Our soaking in the Scriptures allows them to penetrate our hearts.

12. A Gold Coin

We've chosen God's Word as our heritage, our treasure. Only this isn't earthly treasure that we've chosen, it's an eternal one. When we do this, we've found a reason for rejoicing.

Leader's Guide

Chapter 1

1. These questions all have the same answer—the Bible. The Bible is our only source of direct revelation from God. We call it our Scriptures. Our holy book. The very Word of God. And it's as vital to a believer's life as algebra is to a mathematician.

2. "That from childhood you have known the Holy Scriptures, which are able to make you wise for salvation through faith which is in Christ Jesus" (2 Tim. 3:15 NKJV). Paul commends Timothy, who has been taught the Scriptures since he was a small child by his mother and grandmother— both believers. We find, from Paul's comments, that these Scriptures are able to make us wise for salvation through faith. It is from the Bible that we find what we need to know in order to be saved. The Bible is our foundation for faith.

3. There's no need to be ashamed if you've checked several of the boxes. God accepts our feelings. He knows our heart. How you feel now is just where you're starting out. If you've found reading your Bible boring in the past, perhaps we can find some ways to make it more interesting to you. If you've found what you read confusing, perhaps we can point you to the tools you need to unravel the meaning you're searching for. If you find a tendency to think the Scriptures far too outdated for today's life, perhaps we can help you learn to make practical applications.

4. All of us have a longing in our hearts to understand the Bible. We feel a drawing towards the Scriptures in our hearts. But good intentions don't always go very far in getting things done. There may be a boatload of reasons why we've never gotten started. But this is our chance to study with some purpose.

5. "In the beginning was the Word, and the Word was with God, and the Word was God. He was in the beginning with God" (John 1:1–2 NKJV). This passage tells us that the Word was with God in the beginning. Not only that, the Word was God! Now don't worry if that little paradox makes you say, "Huh?" A little digging around will help us understand what all of this means.

6. *John 17:5*—"And now, O Father, glorify Me together with Yourself, with the glory which I had with You before the world was" (NKJV). Here we find a verse that echoes the fact that the Word (Jesus) was with God before the world was created, and that He shared in God's glory—making Him equal with God. 1 *John 1:1*—"That which was from the beginning, which we have heard, which we have seen with our eyes, which we have looked upon, and our hands have handled concerning the Word of life" (NKJV). John is laying the groundwork for his letter by telling us that he was an eyewitness of Jesus and all that He did here on earth. He calls Jesus the Word of life. *Revelation 19:13*—"He was clothed with a robe dipped in blood, and His name is called The Word of God" (NKJV). In John's revelation, he describes for us the Second Coming of Christ, and describes His appearance in this context. In this particular verse, we are told again that His name is called The Word of God.

7. "And the Word became flesh and dwelt among us, and we beheld His glory, the glory as of the only begotten of the Father, full of grace and truth" (John 1:14 NKJV). The Word became flesh—that means we're definitely talking about Jesus here. We can see John's description of the Christ unfolding. He calls Jesus the Word. John's telling us something of who Jesus is, where He's come from, and what His attributes are.

8. "For by Him all things were created that are in heaven and that are on earth, visible and invisible, whether thrones or dominions or principalities or powers. All things were created through Him and for Him. And He is before all things, and in Him all things consist" (Col. 1:16–17 NKJV). Did you know that it was Jesus who created everything? When God spoke, it was the Word that created it all.

9. "By faith we understand that the worlds were framed by the word of God, so that the things which are seen were not made of things which are visible" (Heb. 11:3 NKJV). By the Word the worlds were framed. "For this they willfully forget: that by the word of God the heavens were of old, and the earth standing out of water and in the water" (2 Pet. 3:5 NKJV). By the Word, the heavens and earth were created. "By the word of the Lord the heavens were made, And all the host of them by the breath of His mouth" (Ps. 33:6 NKJV). By the Word, by the very breath of His mouth, the heavens were made.

Chapter 2

1. According to the study notes in the NKJV Study Bible, "Doctrine is teaching. Paul highlights correct teaching first . . . .Reproof is conviction. This is not simply a rebuke; it is demonstrating some truth beyond dispute. Correction refers to setting something straight. Instruction refers to the process of training a child. In this list, only one of these terms is oriented to knowledge and information—that is doctrine. The other three in the list involve a change of life. Knowledge that does not change one's life is useless. On the other hand, living without any understanding of who God is and what He expects of us is dangerous."

2. Yes, as a matter of fact it is. Job 32:8: "But there is a spirit in man, And the breath of the Almighty give him understanding" (NKJV). You might think, "Hey! I don't see the word 'inspiration' in that verse!" True. But you see the phrase "breath of the Almighty." Let's do a little more digging.

3. In the *New Illustrated Bible Commentary*, we find out "given by inspiration is literally 'God-breathed.' In this verse, Paul teaches that God was actively involved in the revelation of His truth to the apostles and prophets, who wrote it down." And in the *Believer's Bible Commentary* we find out even more details. "This is one of the most important verses in the Bible on the subject of inspiration. It teaches that the Scriptures are God-breathed. In a miraculous way, He communicated His word to men and led them to write it down for permanent preservation. What they wrote was the very word of God, inspired and infallible. While it is true that the individual literary style of the writer was not destroyed, it is also true that the very words he used were words given to him by the Holy Spirit."

4. I hope wading through all those Greek terms didn't throw you off. According to *Vine's*, the word translated "complete" in 2 Timothy 3:17 is *artios*, which literally means "fitted, complete." The study notes in the NKJV Study Bible add a tidbit. "The study of Scripture will make a believer complete, meaning 'capable' or 'proficient.'"

5. According to the *New Illustrated Bible Commentary*, "Thoroughly equipped means 'fully prepared.' The person who masters the Word of God will never lose his or her way."

6. In *The MacArthur Topical Bible*, there's quite a lengthy entry for good works—three pages worth! Here's a sampling of the entries about good works under the heading *Believers*. They will have good works if they abide in Christ, good works are wrought by God in them, we were created in Christ for good works, we are exhorted to put on good works, we need to be equipped for good works, we should be careful to maintain good works, we should be ready to engage frequently in good works, we should encourage each other to good works, and our good works will follow us after we die.

Chapter 3

1. e, h, a, c, i, b, j, f, d, g

2. "You search the Scriptures, for in them you think you have eternal life; and these are they which testify of Me" (John 5:39 NKJV). The word used here is "search." In this passage, Jesus is speaking to a hostile audience. He says that these people have searched the Scriptures, thinking to find in them a way to eternal life. What He's telling them is that these self-same Scriptures are testifying of Him—Messiah. Jesus is the only way to eternal life, and the Scriptures are pointing to Him, but His detractors refuse to see this. What we can glean here in our own study of the Scriptures is 1) we can search (study) the Scriptures, and 2) the Old Testament testifies of Jesus.

3. "So then faith comes by hearing, and hearing by the word of God" (Rom. 10:17 NKJV). We have faith because we have the Scriptures! They are its sure foundation. So many mock faith, because we believe in something we cannot see or hear or touch. But we do have something tangible—God's Word.

4. "These were more fair-minded than those in Thessalonica, in that they received the word with all readiness, and searched the Scriptures daily to find out whether these things were so. Therefore many of them believed, and also not a few of the Greeks, prominent women as well as men" (Acts 17:11–12 NKJV).

5. Fair-minded, as we find it in the New King James Version, is literally "noble." The Greek word translated "noble" is *eugenes*, which is made up of two parts. The first segment, *euge*, means "well done." The second segment, "genes," simply means person. This term also occurs in Luke 19:17, in the midst of the Parable of the Talents, when the master commends, "Well done, good servant." In this case we see *euge*, "well done," used again. The servant, in his dealings, proved to be levelheaded, wise, sensible, and ultimately reliable. He was a "well done" kind of guy. It's interesting to note that this "well done" also appears in Matthew 25:21—"Well done, good and faithful servant, enter in to the joy of your lord" (NKJV). The Bereans were fair-minded, noble, and worthy of a "well done" commendation for their wise actions.

6. Throughout the Bible, there are two basic words that are used for "receive." The most common is *lambano*, which means, "to lay hold of." For instance, if you were to *lambano* a fish, you would be laying hold of it, or catching it. However this is not the term used in Acts 17:11. The term here is *dechomai*, which can be variously translated, "to gain access to, to receive with hospitality, to bring into one's family, or to educate." Perhaps the best image here is one of adoption. When you adopt a child, you receive it into your home with hospitality. These Bereans listened to the words of Paul, and in receiving them, they adopted them, owned them, internalized them. They are doing with the Word of God what a family does with an adopted child—taking it in and making it their own with gladness.

7. The word translated "readiness" in Acts 17:11 is *prothymia*. This Greek word is made up of two smaller ones. The first segment, *pro*, indicates forward thinking or good thinking. The second segment, which comes from the Greek word *thumos*, indicates a strong passion of the mind or soul. It suggests strong emotions and a readiness of the mind. So these noble (well done!) Bereans not only received (adopted, welcomed) the words of Paul, they also heard these words with a passionate eagerness of mind.

8. The Greek term for "searched" is *anakrino*. The first bit, *ana*, can be variously translated "in the middle of, several, repeatedly, many times." The second part, *krino*, means "to judge, to be critical, to condemn, to call into question." Together these two create *anakrino*, and give the sense of something being scrutinized or interrogated in order to determine its defects or excellence.

Chapter 4

1. "And I brethren, could not speak to you as to spiritual people but as to carnal, as to babies in Christ. I fed you with milk and not with solid food; for until now you were not able to receive it" (1 Cor. 3:1–2 NKJV). Paul is pretty upset with the church at Corinth here. While they should have been growing and maturing in their faith, they'd remained selfish and inconsistent in their walk. Paul considered them mere babies in Christ—newbies.

2. "As newborn babes, desire the pure milk of the word, that you may grow thereby" (1 Pet. 2:2 NKJV). We need to feel our need of God's Word, to long for it as babies do their milk. For it is through taking in and understanding God's Word that we are able to grow and mature in the Christian faith.

3. "For though by this time you ought to be teachers, you need someone to teach you again the first principles of the oracles of God; and you have come to need milk and not solid food. For everyone who partakes

only of milk is unskilled in the word of righteousness, for he is a babe. But solid food belongs to those who are of full age, that is, those who by reason of use have their senses exercised to discern both good and evil" (Heb. 5:13–14 NKJV). Newbies, or babes in Christ, are unable to teach. They only have a grasp of the most basic principles of Scripture—just enough to be saved. Newbies need to grow, moving from milk to meat. This comes by using what they know—applying the principles of Scripture to their lives. They must be able to recognize and choose good over evil.

4. "Or do you not know that your body is the temple of the Holy Spirit, who is in you, whom you have from God, and you are not your own?" (1 Cor. 6:19 NKJV). We have the Holy Spirit right inside ourselves. God sent Him to us when we were saved.

5. g, d, j, a, h, b, f, i, e, c

6. "But the Helper, the Holy Spirit, whom the Father will send in My name, He will teach you all things, and bring to your remembrance all things that I said to you" (John 14:26 NKJV). The Spirit helps us by teaching us about spiritual things. He brought to mind Jesus' words to the disciples, and for us He brings to mind the Scriptures we've committed to memory.

7. "However, when He, the Spirit of truth, has come, He will guide you into all truth; for He will not speak on His own authority, but whatever He hears He will speak; and He will tell you things to come. He will glorify Me, for He will take of what is Mine and declare it to you" (John 16:13–14 NKJV). The Spirit will guide us into all truth.

8. "Prophecy never came by the will of man, but holy men of God spoke as they were moved by the Holy Spirit" (2 Pet. 1:21 NKJV). The men who wrote the books we now call Scripture were moved by the Holy Spirit to write what they wrote. That's why we say Scripture is inspired.

9. "All Scripture is given by inspiration of God, and is profitable for doctrine, for reproof, for correction, for instruction in righteousness, that the man of God may be complete, thoroughly equipped for every good work" (2 Tim. 3:16–17 NKJV). All Scripture came down to us because of

the inspiration of God. Paul goes on to tell us just what those Scriptures are good for! Doctrine, reproof, correction, instruction—everything we need to be equipped!

Chapter 5

1. "Having been born again" (NKJV). "For you have been born again" (NLT). "You have been born again" (NCV). "Your new life is not like your old life" (MSG). Very similar wording here in all translations—good.

2. "Not of corruptible seed" (NKJV). "Your life did not come from your earthly parents because the life they give you will end in death" (NLT). "This new life did not come from something that dies" (NCV). "Your old birth came from mortal sperm" (MSG). These days, corruptible gives us the idea of something that is weak-willed and easily led. A corruptible man can be bribed or bullied into all manner of sin. But that's not what corruptible means in this biblical context. Here, corruptible refers to a thing that is temporary, passing, perishable. Bananas are "corruptible" because they change from bright yellow to black mush in a matter of days. Peter says our salvation is not of a corruptible nature. It's interesting that the *New Living Translation* and *The Message* equate "corruptible seed" with earthly conception.

3. "But incorruptible" (NKJV). "But this new life will last forever" (NLT). "From something that cannot die" (NCV). "A life conceived by God himself!" (MSG). Ah! Not corruptible, but incorruptible. Our salvation is something lasting, unfading, eternal!

4. "Through the word of God" (NKJV). "It comes from . . . the word of God" (NLT). "You were born again through God's living message" (NCV). "Your new birth comes from God's living Word" (MSG).

5. "Which lives and abides forever" (NKJV). "Eternal, living" (NLT). "That continues forever" (NCV). Our new life is as eternal as the Word from which we learned of it.

6. Along with using the cross-references in your Bible, this comparing of various translations is one of the simplest aids to Bible study we have. Hunt around the house. How many versions do you own? Just make sure you have at least one formal equivalent among your translations so that you have a kind of baseline to start from.

Chapter 6

1. Balak thought he was being very clever, for he'd found a prophet of God and planned to use that prophet against God's own people. All he needed to do was buy the prophet's cooperation, and he'd pull off the double-cross of the century. (That, dear ladies, is what we call a paraphrase!) The prophet Balaam was tempted to accept the bribe Balak offered, but when it came down to the crucial moment, Balaam couldn't do it. "Then Balaam answered and said to the servants of Balak, 'Though Balak were to give me his house full of silver and gold, I could not go beyond the word of the Lord my God, to do less or more" (Num. 22:18 NKJV). And again, "I could not go beyond the word of the Lord, to do good or bad of my own will. What the Lord says, that I must speak" (Num. 24:13 NKJV).

2. "Making the word of God of no effect through your tradition which you have handed down" (Mark 7:13 NKJV). The Pharisees had a tradition that provided a loophole, allowing them to ignore one of God's commandments—one of the Ten Commandments, in fact. The Pharisees felt justified, but Jesus was scandalized.

3. "For we are not, as so many, peddling the word of God; but as of sincerity, but as from God, we speak in the sight of God in Christ" (2 Cor. 2:17 NKJV). Even then, in the earliest days of Christianity, there were those who preached for profit. Paul calls them peddlers. They used religion for personal gain.

4. "Not walking in craftiness nor handling the word of God deceitfully, but by manifestation of the truth commending ourselves to every man's

conscience in the sight of God" (2 Cor. 4:2 NKJV). Paul didn't have any sly motives in teaching God's Word. He didn't handle Scripture deceitfully, with hidden, selfish motives behind a ministry front.

5. "As also in all his epistles, speaking in them of these things, in which are some things hard to understand, which untaught and unstable people twist to their own destruction, as they do also the rest of the Scriptures" (2 Pet. 3:16 NKJV). According to the study notes in the NKJV Study Bible, "Untaught refers to one whose mind is untrained and undisciplined in habits of thought. Unstable refers to one whose conduct is not properly established on the truths of God's Word. "

6. According to *Nelson's New Illustrated Bible Commentary*, "Note that Peter equates the letters of Paul with the rest of the Scriptures, indicating that Peter considered the apostle Paul's writings to be the Word of God. Note that Peter considers Paul's writings on the end times to be hard to understand. This should be a comfort to each of us who attempts to interpret the writings of Paul on the coming of Christ. Even Peter found them difficult.

7. "Jesus answered and said to them, 'You are mistaken, not knowing the Scriptures nor the power of God" (Matt. 22:29 NKJV). What are your strongest convictions based on? Do you know how to back up your beliefs based on the truths of the Scriptures? Do you speak from reservoirs of understanding, or from ignorance?

8. "Knowing this first, that no prophecy of Scripture is of any private interpretation" (2 Pet. 1:20 NKJV). According to *Nelson's New Illustrated Bible Commentary*, "Although some have taken this phrase to mean that no individual Christian has the right to interpret prophecy for himself or herself, the context and the Greek word for *interpretation* indicates another meaning for the verse. The Greek word for *interpretation* can also mean "origin." In the context of verse 21, it is clear that Peter is speaking of Scripture's origin from God Himself and not the credentials of the one

who interprets it. There is no private source for the Bible; the prophets did not supply their own solutions or explanations to the mysteries of life. Rather, God spoke through them; He alone is responsible for what is written in Scripture. This is why Christians should study the Bible diligently. It is God's Word."

9. "You shall not add to the word which I command you, not take anything from it, that you may keep the commandments of the Lord your God which I command you" (Deut. 4:2 NKJV). "Whatever I command you, be careful to observe it; you shall not add to it nor take away from it" (Deut. 12:32 NKJV). "For I testify to everyone who hears the words of the prophecy of this book: If anyone adds to these things, God will add to him the plagues that are written in this book; and if anyone takes away from the words of the book of this prophecy, God shall take away his part from the Book of Life, from the holy city, and from the things which are written in this book" (Rev. 22:18, 19 NKJV).

Chapter 7

1. Pure, proven, right. God's Word is all these things.

2. 1 John 2:14—the word of God *abides*. 1 Thessalonians 2:13—the word of God effectively *works* in you. 1 Peter 1:25—the word of the Lord *endures* forever.

3. "The Scripture cannot be broken" (John 10:35 NKJV). This is a strong statement of the inerrancy of the Scriptures. "The word of God is not chained" (2 Tim. 2:9 NKJV). Nothing we might try can hinder or confine the Word of God.

4. "Many of those who heard the word *believed*" (Acts 4:4 NKJV). "They were filled with the Holy Spirit, and they *spoke* the word of God with boldness" (Acts 4:31 NKJV). "They were *glad* and *glorified* the word of the Lord" (Acts 13:48 NKJV). "Have *tasted* the good word of God" (Heb. 6:5 NKJV).

5. Positive attributes listed: undefiled (v. 1), diligently (v. 4), directed (v. 5), uprightness (v. 7), open eyes (v. 18). Positive actions listed: walk (v. 1), keep (v. 2), seek wholeheartedly (v. 2), look into (v. 6), praise (v. 7), cleanse (v. 9), take heed (v. 9), sought (v. 10), hidden the word (v. 11), declared (v. 13), rejoiced (v. 14), meditate (v. 15), contemplate (v. 15), delight (v. 16), longing (v. 20), meditates (v. 23), delights (v. 24).

6. Negative attitudes listed: ashamed (v. 6), reproach (v. 22), contempt (v. 22). Negative actions listed: do iniquity (v. 3), wander (v. 10), sin (v. 11), forget (v. 16).

7. God directs (v. 5), teaches (v. 12), deals bountifully (v. 17), opens our eyes (v. 18), removes our reproach (v. 23), counsels (v. 24).

8. God also forsakes (v. 8), hides (v. 19), rebukes (v. 21).

9. God's Word is variously referred to as the Law of the Lord, His testimonies, His ways, and also Your precepts, Your statutes, Your commandments, Your judgments, and Your word.

Chapter 8

1. "Hold fast the pattern of sound words which you have heard from me, in faith and love which are in Christ Jesus" (2 Tim. 1:13 NKJV).

2. According to *Vine's*, the word translated "pattern" in 2 Timothy 1:13 is *hupotuposis*, which can literally be translated "outline" or "sketch." Hey! Outline! According to the **Believer's Bible Commentary**, "It is not just that he is to be loyal to the truth of God's word, but that he is to cling to the very expressions by which this truth is conveyed. Perhaps an illustration of this might help. In our day, it is sometimes suggested that we should abandon such old-fashioned expressions as 'being born again' or 'the blood of Jesus.' People want to use more sophisticated language. But there is a subtle danger here. In abandoning the scriptural mode of expression, they often abandon the very truths which are communicated by these expressions. Therefore, Timothy should hold fast the very pattern of healthful words." God chose His words carefully before handing them down to us, and they are the outline we need to live by.

3. A very simple outline of this passage might look something like this:

- Christ
  - ~ Loved the church
  - ~ Gave Himself for it
    - So that He might
    - ~ Sanctify
    - ~ Cleanse it
      - With the washing of water by the word
      - ~So that He might present it
        - Not having spot
        - Not having wrinkle
        - Or any such thing
        - Holy
        - Without blemish

4. A simple outline of the sentence structure of Hebrews 1:1–3 might look something like this.

- God
  - ~ spoke
  - At various times
  - In different ways
  - In times past
  - To the fathers
  - By the prophets
    - ~ Has spoken
      - In these last days
      - To us
      - By His Son
        - ~ Whom He has appointed Heir of all things
        - ~ Through whom He made the worlds
        - ~ Who being the brightness of His glory
        - ~ The express image of His person
        - ~ Upholding all things
          - By the word of His power
            - ~ He purged our sins
            - ~ Sat down at the right hand of the Majesty on high

5. An outline of 2 Peter 3:5–7 might look something like this:
- By the Word of God
  - ~ The heavens were of old (created)
  - ~ The earth standing out of the water (created)
  - ~ The earth standing under water, being flooded (destroyed)
  - ~ The heavens and the earth are kept in store (future destruction)

6. "By the word of the Lord the heavens were made, and all the host of them by the breath of His mouth" (Ps. 33:6 NKJV). All of heaven and every angel that lives there came to be by the word of the Lord.

7. "By faith we understand that the worlds were framed by the word of God, so that the things which are seen were not made of things which are visible" (Heb. 11:3 NKJV). We know by faith that God created this world of ours. He spoke everything we see into being.

8. An outline of Luke 8:4–15 might look something like this:
- A Sower went out to sow his seed
  - ~ Some fell by the wayside
    - It was trampled down
    - The birds of the air devoured it
  - ~ Some fell on rock
    - It sprang up quickly
    - It withered away for lack of moisture
  - ~ Some fell among thorns
    - The thorns sprang up with it
    - It was choked
  - ~ Some fell on good ground
    - Sprang up
    - Yielded a crop a hundredfold
    - The seed is the Word of God
  - ~ Those by wayside
    - Hear the word
    - Devil comes and takes the word out of their hearts
  - Prevents them from believing
  - They are not saved

~ The ones on the rock
  - Hear the word
  - Receive the word with joy
  - Have no root
  - Believe for a while
  - In time of temptation, they fall away
~ The ones in the thorns
  - Hear the word
  - The word is choked out
~ By cares
~ By riches
~ By pleasures of life
  - They bring no fruit to maturity
~ The ones that fell on good ground
  - Heard the Word with a noble and good heart
  - Keep it
  - Bear fruit with patience

9. Here is the list I would create from this passage:

1. I love Your Word.
2. Your Word is my meditation all day long.
3. Your Word has made me wiser than my enemies.
4. Your Word has given me more understanding than teachers.
5. Your Word has given me more understanding than the ancients.
6. Your Word restrains me from evil.
7. Your Word will be kept.
8. I will never depart from Your Word.
9. You Yourself have taught me.
10. Your words are sweet to me.
11. Your words have given me understanding.
12. Your Word has taught me to hate false ways.

10. According to *The MacArthur Topical Bible*, these are the names for the Scriptures that we find in the Bible—the Word, the Word of God, the Word of Christ, the Word of truth, the Holy Scriptures, the Scripture of truth, the Book, the Book of the Lord, the Book of the Law, the Law of the Lord, the Sword of the Spirit, and the Oracles of God.

Chapter 9

1. In our handy-dandy English dictionary, we discover that diligent means, "marked by persevering, painstaking effort." The Greek word translated "diligent" in the *New King James Version* of our Bibles is *spoudozo*, which literally means "to exert oneself." It gives the sense of being proactive or determined in getting things done. The root of *spoudozo is speudo*, which means, "to desire tenaciously." So you see, the term gives the idea not merely of an attitude of the mind, but an active follow-through of the person. So when Paul tells us to be diligent in presenting ourselves to God, he's not talking about our good intentions, but of our exertions in bringing that desire into reality.

2. The Greek word translated "present" is *paristemi*. This word is made up of two smaller segments, *par* meaning "with, beside, by, or near" and *istemi*, "to stand." So we have the idea of standing beside something. There's a nice word picture we can bring out here. Consider the bride on her wedding day. Her father stands beside her, walking her down the aisle, to present her to her new husband, who will be the man to stand beside her from then on. The father presents his daughter to her new husband. We are to present ourselves to God.

3. *Approved* comes from the Greek word *dokimos*, which means, "approved, accepted, pleasing." According to Don Barnhouse's commentary, this word comes from ancient Athens and the banking industry. Back then, all money was minted from metal. The coins were created by pouring precious metals into mold, letting them cool, then smoothing the uneven edges down before putting them into circulation. Dishonest men took these metal coins and shaved them down slightly, collecting the trimmings and passing along coins that were a little smaller and thinner than they should have been. More than eighty laws were passed in ancient Greece to prevent this practice. Men of honor would only put full-weighted coins into circulation. They refused to accept or pass on the coins which had been shaved. These honest men were called *dokimos*—"approved."

4. The word used in the Greek for "rightly dividing" is *orthotomeo*. Again, this is a compound word. The first section comes from the word *orthos*, which means, "straight, upright, not crooked." The second, *tomos*, is a derivative from *temno*, which means, "to cut." Together, this gives the idea of precision, and of making clean incisions with no ragged edges. The opposite of this would be *kopto*, which means, "to hack." The implication of "rightly dividing" is correct and careful handling.

5. Dwell comes from the Greek word *enoikeo*, which comes from *en*, "in" and *oikos*, "house." Literally "in house," *enoikeo* is translated "to live in" or "to dwell." Metaphorically, *Dwelling* points to influence. Would you act differently if your pastor moved into your home for a week? We'd be as good as gold! What if you had a suspected murderer living with you? We'd be locked in our bedroom! The one who lives with us influences our behavior, our actions, our decisions. When the Word of God is dwelling in us, it influences us for good.

6. *Richly* comes from the Greek word *plousios*, which is a simple adverb meaning, "full, abounding, to the fullest extent." In other words, if you were pouring water into a cup, and doing it to the fullest extent, you would keep pouring until the water spills over the edge.

7. The Greek word translated "admonishing," is *noutheteo*, from which we get the nouthetic in *nouthetic* counseling (Bible-based, as opposed to psychology-based). This word can be translated, "exhort; admonish." *Admonishing* is warning someone when they're in need of change. It's taking someone aside and gently but firmly pointing out their areas of weakness and fault, then telling them what the Bible has to say about it.

8. "For assuredly, I say to you, till heaven and earth pass away, one jot or one tittle will by no means pass from the law till all is fulfilled" (Matt. 5:18 NKJV). All the things we read in our Bible—promises and prophecies alike—will happen. Not one jot or tittle will be left out.

9. *Jot* refers to the Hebrew word *yod*, which is the smallest letter of the Hebrew alphabet. It's comparable with an apostrophe or a comma—just a small curved mark. A tittle is the smallest stroke in a Hebrew letter. It's little more than a flyspeck. What Jesus is saying is that even the smallest letter and the smallest part of a letter won't be left out. All will be fulfilled before the end. Every "t" will be crossed, and every "i" dotted!

Chapter 10

1. "Cause me to hear Your lovingkindness in the morning, for in You do I trust; cause me to know the way in which I should walk, for I lift up my soul to You" (Ps. 143:8 NKJV). David wants to hear God's lovingkindness to know how to walk before God.

2. "To him the doorkeeper opens, and the sheep hear his voice; and he calls his own sheep by name and leads them out" (John 10:3 NKJV). Sheep spend all their days under their shepherd's care, and so they learn to know and trust the voice of their shepherd. The shepherd, in turn, recognizes each and every one of his sheep, and can call to them by name. "My sheep hear My voice, and I know them, and they follow Me" (John 10:27 NKJV). We are the Lord's and we can recognize His voice. We, like sheep, should trust and follow Him.

3. "But they did not *obey* nor *incline* their *ear*, but made their *neck stiff*, that they might not *hear* nor *receive instruction*" (Jer. 17:23 NKJV). "For the *hearts* of this people have *grown dull*. Their *ears* are *hard* of *hearing*, and their *eyes* they have *closed*, lest they should *see* with their *eyes* and *hear* with their *ears*, lest they should *understand* with their *hearts* and *turn*" (Matt. 13:15 NKJV). "Today, if you will *hear* His *voice*, do not *harden* your *hearts* as in the *rebellion*" (Heb. 3:15 NKJV). The attitude is called by different names in the Bible—a hard heart, a stiff neck—but either way, it's an unwillingness to obey God. For whatever reason, there are times when we'd rather do our own thing than what we know is right. When we deliberately turn a deaf ear to our conscience and a blind eye to the Word, we're rebelling.

4. "So they come to you as people do, they sit before you as My people, and they hear your words, but they do not do them; for with their mouth they show much love, but their hearts pursue their own gain. Indeed you are to them as a very lovely song of one who has a pleasant voice and can play well on an instrument; for they hear your words, but they do not do them" (Ezek. 33:31–32 NKJV). Even worse than out and out rebels are the hypocrites. They're the ones who say they love God, and make a show of serving Him, but do their own thing no matter what the Bible says.

5. "Blessed are your eyes for they see, and your ears for they hear" (Matt. 13:16 NKJV). Jesus was always saying, "He who has ears to hear, let him hear!" (Luke 8:8 NKJV). When the people who followed Jesus heard His messages with eagerness, understanding, and teachable hearts, He called them blessed.

6. "More than that, blessed are those who hear the word of God and keep it" (Luke 11:28 NKJV). Even more blessed than those who can hear Jesus' message and understand it are those who hear it, understand it, and then go out and obey it! Hearing isn't enough. It must be followed up with obedience.

7. "Not the hearers of the law are just in the sight of God, but the doers of the law will be justified" (Rom. 2:13 NKJV). Just knowing the law isn't enough. We need to do as God commands in order to be justified. Have you ever wondered just what He asks of us? That would be an excellent theme to pursue through the Scriptures!

8. "Be doers of the word, and not hearers only, deceiving yourselves" (James 1:22 NKJV). We're fooling ourselves if we spend all our time studying the Bible, but never apply what we learn to our own lives. Allow the Spirit to convict. Hear him! Then, with His help and power, obey!

9. "Blessed is he who reads and those who hear the words of this prophecy, and keep those things which are written in it; for the time is near" (Rev. 1:3 NKJV). The blessing is for those who hear and obey what is written. The warning is that the time is near. Don't put off until another day what you know you should be doing now.

Chapter 11

1. "Give ear to my words, O Lord, Consider my meditation" (Ps. 5:1 NKJV). "Hear my voice, O God, in my meditation" (Ps. 64:1 NKJV). Meditation in the psalms could also be translated *contemplation*. *Meditate* means, "to mumble" or "to speak to oneself." *Meditation* means focusing your mind on the Scriptures, running over them inside your head, and talking to yourself about them.

2. "I call to remembrance my song in the night; I meditate within my heart, and my spirit makes diligent search" (Ps. 77:6). "My eyes are awake through the night watches, that I may meditate on Your word" (Ps. 119:148 NKJV). According to *Nelson's New Illustrated Bible Commentary*, "The Jews, like the Greeks and the Romans, divided the night into military watches instead of hours. Accompanying the prevailing prayer of the psalmist was a meditation in the Word of God. Prayer and reading the Word preceded the dawning of the day and continued unto the watches of the night. That is the secret of getting a hold on God."

3. "His delight is in the law of the Lord, and in His law he meditates day and night" (Ps. 1:2 NKJV). Here, David talks about more than just peace and quiet.

Sure, it'd be nice if we could have peace and quiet for our meditations. But in reality, we live in a busy, noisy world. We need to make meditation such a second nature, that our hearts are always pondering over the things we're learning in the Word.

4. "This Book of the Law shall not depart from your mouth, but you shall meditate in it day and night, that you may observe to do according to all that is written in it. For then you will make your way prosperous, and then you will have good success" (Josh. 1:8 NKJV). Joshua is to make himself so familiar with the Law that it's always running through his mind. Why? Because in doing what God commands, he's promised success and prosperity as the new leader of God's people.

5. c, g, a, e, h, b, f, d

6. "Let the words of my mouth and the meditation of my heart be acceptable in Your sight, O Lord, my strength and my Redeemer" (Ps. 19:14 NKJV). "May my meditation be sweet to Him; I will be glad in the Lord" (Ps. 104:34 NKJV). David wants his meditations to be acceptable, even sweet to the Lord.

7. "Finally, brethren, whatever things are true, whatever things are noble, whatever things are just, whatever things are pure, whatever things are lovely, whatever things are of good report, if there is any virtue and if there is anything praiseworthy—meditate on these things" (Phil. 4:8

NKJV). Now here's an excellent list. It would be fascinating to do a word study on each of these adjectives!

8. "Meditate on these things; give yourself entirely to them, that your progress may be evident to all" (1 Tim. 4:15 NKJV). Meditation may seem like a purely internal action—one of reflection and contemplation. But Paul assures us that when we meditate and internalize the truths of God's Word, our lives will be changed. And those changes will be apparent to everyone.

Chapter 12

1. "Though I have the *gift* of *prophecy*, and *understand* all *mysteries* and all *knowledge*, and though I have all *faith*, so that I could *remove mountains*, but have not *love*, I am *nothing*" (1 Cor. 13:2 NKJV).

2. "So shall My word be that goes forth from My mouth; it shall not return to Me void, but it shall accomplish what I please, and it shall prosper in the thing for which I sent it" (Is. 55:11 NKJV).

3. "Sanctify them by Your truth. Your word is truth" (John 17:17 NKJV). The Word sanctifies us. What does that mean? According to *Nelson's New Illustrated Bible Dictionary*, "Sanctify means 'to set apart.' There are two ways to understand this statement: (1) as separate for holiness, or (2) as set apart for service. According to the first view, Jesus was praying not only that the disciples should be kept from evil, but that they should advance in holiness. However in verse 18, sanctification seems to refer to the disciples' mission, indicating that sanctify may also mean that Jesus was setting apart His disciples for this." Have you ever wondered what God has set you apart for?

4. We've already covered this verse in a previous lesson, but it deserves repeating! "How can a young man cleanse his way? By taking heed according to Your word" (Ps. 119:9 NKJV). You want to know how to please God, to live right, to do good? Here's where we can learn!

5. "And now, brethren, I commend you to God and to the word of His grace, which is able to build you up and give you an inheritance among all

those who are sanctified" (Acts 20:32 NKJV). Let's compare a few translations on this one. "I entrust you to God and the word of his grace—his message that is able to build you up and give you an inheritance with all those he has set apart for himself" (NLT). "Now I am putting you into the care of God and the message about his grace. It is able to give you strength, and it will give you the blessings God has for all his holy people" (NCV). "Now I'm turning you over to God, our marvelous God whose gracious Word can make you into what he wants you to be and give you everything you could possibly need in this community of holy friends" (MSG).

6. "By them Your servant is warned, and in keeping them there is great reward" (Ps. 19:11 NKJV). This is admonition. This is a very cool passage about God's Word! According to *Nelson's New Illustrated Bible Commentary*, "This passage presents six words for the Law of God—law, testimony, statutes, commandment, fear, and judgments; six evaluations of the law—perfect, sure, right, pure, clean, and true; and six results—converting the soul, making wise the simple, rejoicing the heart, enlightening the eyes, enduring forever, and righteous altogether." Wow!

7. "The statutes of the Lord are right, rejoicing the heart; the commandment of the Lord is pure, enlightening the eyes" (Ps. 19:8 NKJV). "Your testimonies I have taken as a heritage forever, for they are the rejoicing of my heart" (Ps. 119:111 NKJV). We shall rejoice! And I love the wording that says we've taken the Word as our heritage. That would be an excellent topic for a journal entry!

8. "For whatever things were written before were written for our learning, that we through the patience and comfort of the Scriptures might have hope" (Rom. 15:4 NKJV). The Bible was written for our learning. It gives us patience. It gives us comfort. It gives us hope. According to the *Nelson's New Illustrated Bible Commentary*, "Through patience (endurance) and the comfort (or encouragement) of Scripture, believers learn that they have hope. In this case, if strong believers are patient with the scruples of the weak, they have hope of being rewarded."

130